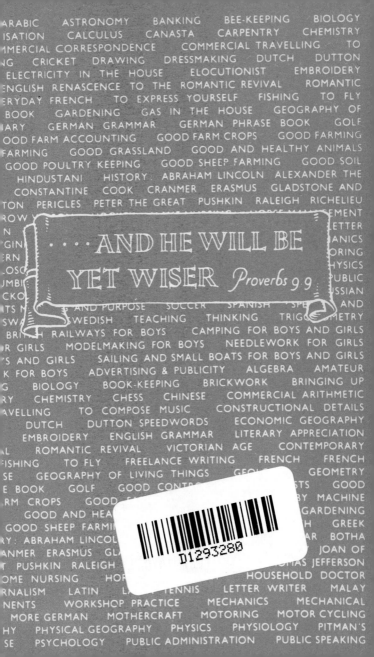

THE TEACH YOURSELF BOOKS
EDITED BY LEONARD CUTTS

TURKISH

TEACH YOURSELF

TURKISH

By

G. L. LEWIS

M.A., D.Phil.

*Senior Lecturer in Islamic Studies
in the University of Oxford*

THE ENGLISH UNIVERSITIES PRESS LTD

102 NEWGATE STREET

LONDON, E.C.1

First printed 1953
This impression 1959

Printed in Great Britain for the English Universities Press, Limited,
by Richard Clay and Company, Ltd., Bungay, Suffolk

INTRODUCTION

TURKISH is a member of the Turkic branch of the Altaic family of languages, spoken by some fifty million people, from the south-east of Europe to the upper reaches of the Yenisei and the borders of China. The languages of this branch do not differ among themselves anything like as much as the languages of our branch of the Indo-European family. English, Dutch and Norwegian are all Germanic, but this fact would be small comfort to the Londoner who suddenly found himself in Amsterdam or Oslo. On the other hand, anyone who has mastered the contents of this book would find little difficulty in making himself understood in Adrianople, in the Turkish-speaking parts of Cyprus, in Chinese Turkestan or Samarkand.

Those who require a knowledge of Turkish for commercial, military, diplomatic or scholarly purposes will need no persuasion to awaken their interest. But there is a reason of another sort for learning the language. The structure of Turkish is simple and logical (it has only one anomalous verb and only one irregular noun); it is, moreover, quite different from the structure of the Indo-European and Semitic languages. Anyone who is seeking a new form of intellectual stimulus will find it a refreshing change to see how Turkish-speakers clothe the ordinary human thoughts and feelings in a completely new garb. Take for example this sentence: ' The book which I have bought for you is on the table.' The shape of this sentence remains the same in French, German, Spanish, Greek and even Arabic. But in Turkish it becomes: ' You-for buy-in-the-past-pertaining-to-me book, table's surface-thereof-at is.'

Turkish is an agglutinating language. A Turkish word consists of an unchanging root and one or more suffixes, each adding one idea to that of the root. For instance, *lingua* in Latin means ' the tongue ', *linguarum* ' of the tongues ', and it is not possible to say which of the added letters carries the idea of plurality and which the meaning ' of '. Nor is a knowledge of this form *linguarum* of any assistance if we wish to translate ' of the tongue ' (*linguæ*) or ' of the seas ' (*marium*). In Turkish, on the other hand, we add *-ler* to indicate the plural and *-in* to express ' of '. So, given that ' tongue ' is *dil* and ' sea ' is *deniz*, we can at once translate ' of the tongue ' *(dilin)*, ' the tongues ' *(diller)*, ' of the tongues ' *(dillerin)*, ' of the seas ' *(denizlerin)* and so on. The same principle is followed throughout the language, so that if one opens a Turkish book at random one will see words like : *elbisemizle*, ' with our clothes ', *gelemiyecektik*, ' we should have been unable to come '; *hürmetsizliklerine*, ' to their lack of respect '. Although the beginner may require several months of practice before he can agglutinate freely in conversation, he will find ample compensation in the ease with which the suffixes enable him to build new words from the roots he already knows.

Until 1928, Turkish was written in the Arabic script, which was inadequate to convey the sounds of Turkish. Thus the Arabic equivalents of the letters *k-w-r-k* stood for no fewer than seven completely different words, now written *kürk*, *kürek*, *gevrek*, *gürek*, *görek*, *körük* and *körün*. The need for a reform had long been discussed, but it took the enlightened despotism of Mustafa Kemal to introduce the Latin alphabet to Turkey and to outlaw the old Arabic script from public life. At the same time, official support was given to the move to rid the language of the numerous Arabic and Persian words which it had adopted over a period of centuries and to replace them by ' genuine Turkish ' words, some resurrected from old texts, some imported from other Turkic languages, some constructed on the analogy of existing words, but a great many simply taken into the written language from the spoken language.

It is easy to poke fun at this policy, but in favour of it it must be said that the immense gulf which existed in the Ottoman Empire, between the language of the educated few and the language of the people, is intolerable in a democratic country. The language reform has done much to unite the Turks linguistically. Nothing is to be gained by adopting the ostrich-attitude and saying : ' *Okul* (" school ") is a ridiculous hybrid, out of the Turkish *oku-* " to read ", by the French *école*. We shall ignore it and continue to use the good old Ottoman word *mektep*.' Turkish children nowadays don't go to *mektep*; they go to *okul*.

Hagopian's *Ottoman-Turkish Conversation-Grammar*, published in 1907, devoted 215 pages to Turkish and 161 pages to Arabic and Persian. The student of modern Turkish has no more need to learn Arabic and Persian than the foreigner studying English has to learn Latin and Greek.

The aim of this book is to present a picture of the Turkish language as it is now generally spoken in Istanbul and written by the best contemporary Turkish stylists. For the most part the ' pen of the janissary's aunt ' type of sentence has been avoided; nearly all the examples have been chosen from modern Turkish books and newspapers.

It is not possible in a book of this size to give exhaustive word-lists, nor indeed is it desirable, because very few people are capable of learning a language by memorizing in advance all the words they are likely to need. An appendix of military terms has, however, been included, much of the information in which is not to be found in any other work. There is also a list of essential verbs which the reader will need to know, whether his business in Turkey concerns tobacco, Hittite tombs, microfilms of Arabic manuscripts or airfields.

My thanks are due to four people who were ungrudging of their help and encouragement to me in the writing of this book : to my wife, whose idea it was, to my friend and teacher Mr. Fahir İz, Lecturer in Turkish at the School of Oriental and African Studies in the University of London, who read the work in proof and made some valuable suggestions for its improvement, and to Mr. G. G. Arthur of H. M. Foreign Service and Major P. A. T. Halliday, Royal Hampshire Regiment, who both assisted greatly in the preparation of the Appendix.

I should like also to pay tribute to the skill and care shown by the staff of the English Universities Press Ltd., and their printers, Messrs. Richard Clay and Company Ltd., in dealing with a difficult manuscript.

G. L. Lewis

Oxford.
  April 1953.

CONTENTS

THE ALPHABET

The Turkish alphabet is made up of eight vowels and twenty-one consonants. For quickness of reference a rough guide to pronunciation is given against each letter. It is essential to supplement these indications by reading carefully the more detailed notes which follow.

Letter		Name	Approximate pronunciation
A	a	a	as in French *avoir*, Northern English *man*
B	b	be	as in English
C	c	ce	*j* in *jam*
Ç	ç	çe	*ch* in *church*
D	d	de	as in English
E	e	e	as in *bed*
F	f	fe	as in English
G	g	ge	as in *goat*
*	ğ	yumuşak ge	lengthens a preceding vowel
H	h	he	as in *house*
I	ı	ı	something like the *u* in *radium*
İ	i	i	as in *pit*
J	j	je	as in French *jour*, like *s* in *leisure*
K	k	ke, ka	as in *king*
L	l	le	as in English
M	m	me	,, ,,
N	n	ne	,, ,,
O	o	o	like French *eau*
Ö	ö	ö	as in German *König*, French *eu* in *deux*
P	p	pe	as in English
R	r	re	as in *ribbon*
S	s	se	as in *sing*
Ş	ş	şe	*sh* in *shall*
T	t	te	as in English
U	u	u	as in *push*
Ü	ü	ü	as in German *Führer*, French *u* in *tu*
V	v	ve	as in English
Y	y	ye	as in *yet*
Z	z	ze	as in English

* *Yumuşak ge* (' soft *g* ') never occurs at the beginning of a word.

11

THE SOUNDS OF TURKISH

1. The notes which follow are not intended to be an exhaustive account of Turkish phonetics, but to help the student to attain an intelligible pronunciation without a native teacher. In this connection, it is worth remembering that there are regular short-wave broadcasts in Turkish, not only from Ankara but also from London and in the Voice of America programmes.

A minimum of phonetic symbols has been used in the descriptions of the sounds, so that the reader who knows nothing of phonetics will not be at a disadvantage.

VOWELS

2. VOWEL LENGTH

As a rule, Turkish vowels are short; for example, *i* ordinarily has the sound heard in the English *bit* [i], not that heard in *machine* [i:].

The exceptions are: (1) short vowels are lengthened under certain conditions when followed by *ğ* or *y* (see §§ 19, 32). (2) In some Arabic and Persian loan-words an original long vowel is retained. Such vowels will be marked long in the Vocabularies thus: *muhārebe*, ' war '. See also § 64.

3. CLASSIFICATION OF VOWELS

The differences between vowels are largely differences in tongue-position. Phoneticians speak of front or back vowels, the former pronounced with the middle of the tongue raised towards the highest part of the palate, the latter with the back of the tongue raised towards the velum (the soft back part of the palate). According to the amount of this raising of the tongue, vowels are described as high, higher-mid, lower-mid or low. Another distinction is between rounded and unrounded vowels, depending on whether or not the sound is produced with rounded, protruded lips. These terms must be kept in mind for when we come to deal with Vowel Harmony (§ 36).

4. *a*

Generally represents the low, unrounded, back vowel [ɑ], much the same as the *a* in the French *avoir* or the Northern

English pronunciation of *man*. When long, it is pronounced like *a* in *father*.

Examples: *yasak*, ' forbidden '; *adam*, ' man '; *âdil* [ɑːdil], ' just '.

In some words, mostly of non-Turkish origin, *a* represents the low, unrounded, front vowel [a], much as in *cat*.

Examples: *anne* [annɛ], ' mother '; *lâzım* [laːzïm], ' necessary '.

5. *e*

Usually the lower-mid front vowel [ɛ], much as in the English *met*.

Examples: *evet*, ' yes '; *ben*, ' I '.

Sometimes it represents the higher-mid front [e] (the French *é*), notably when lengthened, the resulting sound being the vowel of English *they*, but without the final *i*-glide heard in this word.

Examples: *teyze* [teːzɛ], ' maternal aunt '; *tesir* [teːsir], ' effect '.

6. *ı*

The high, unrounded, intermediate vowel [ï], which does not occur in English. If you spread your lips as if to say *easy* and then pronounce the first syllable of the word *cushion*, you will be saying the Turkish word *kış*, ' winter '. Alternatively, try to pronounce the syllable *dr*, with the shortest possible vowel between the two consonants: the result should be very close to the Turkish *dır*, ' is '.

Examples: *karı*, ' woman '; *rıhtım*, ' quay '; *kapıda*, ' at the gate '.

7. *i*

The low, unrounded, front vowel as in *pit* or, when long, as in *machine*.

Examples: *ip*, ' thread '; *bir*, ' one '; *iğne* [iːnɛ], ' needle '.

8. *o*

Usually represents the higher-mid rounded back vowel [o], like the French *eau*, a clipped version of the vowel-sound in the English *moat*, but without the final *u*-glide heard in this word.

Examples: *on*, ' ten '; *ot*, ' grass '; *oğlan* [oːɬɑn], ' boy '.

In words borrowed from French and in Turkish words

beginning with *n* or *l*, *o* represents the lower-mid rounded back vowel [ɔ], as in English *hot* or French *homme*.

Examples: *nokta* [nɔktɑ], ' point '; *Londra* [lɔndrɑ], ' London '.

9. ö

The lower-mid rounded front vowel [œ]. The tongue-position is the same as for [ɛ] (§ 5), but the lips are puckered. The sound is that of German *ö* in *König*, French *eu* in *deux*.

Examples: *ömür*, ' life '; *ördek*, ' duck '.

10. u

Generally represents the high, rounded, back vowel [ʊ] as in *push*, with lips rounded and parted.

Examples: *upuzun*, ' very long '; *uzak*, ' far '.

In some words, particularly those beginning with *l* or *n* followed by *u*, the *u* is pronounced [u], with the back of the tongue raised even closer towards the soft palate than for [ʊ], and the lips only slightly parted, the resulting sound being similar to but shorter than the *oo* in *loom*.

Examples: *numara* [numɑrɑ], ' number '; *nutuk* [nutʊk], ' speech '.

11. ü

The high rounded front vowel [y], the German *ü* in *Führer*, French *u* in *tu*. If you pronounce the English word *itch* with rounded lips, you will be saying the Turkish word *üç*, ' three '.

Examples: *üzüm*, ' grapes '; *yüz*, ' hundred '.

12. â, û, î, aa

(1) As will be explained in §§ 18 and 23, the circumflex accent is written over *a* and *u* to indicate that a preceding *g*, *k* or *l* is palatalized.

(2) Used after these three consonants, the circumflex does not necessarily denote vowel-length. Elsewhere it does. Some writers use it over all long vowels in Arabic and Persian borrowings, but ordinarily it is used only where confusion might otherwise arise. Note especially these three words: *hala* [hɑłɑ], ' paternal aunt '; *hâlâ* [ha:la:], ' yet '; *halâ* [hala:], ' void '.

(3) It follows that when it is necessary to differentiate between long and short *a* after a non-palatalized *g* or *k*, the circumflex cannot be used. Instead, the length of the *a* is shown by writing it twice: *kaatil* [kɑ:til], ' murderer ', but *katil* [kɑtil], ' murder '.

CONSONANTS

13. *b, p*

b and its unvoiced equivalent *p* are not so heavily aspirated as in English; i.e. they are produced with less emission of breath than is heard, for example, in the first syllable of *poppycock*.

Examples: *baba*, ' father '; *pazar*, ' market '.

14. *c*

Exactly like English *j* in *jam*.

Examples: *cep*, ' pocket '; *Cava*, ' Java '.

15. *ç*

Exactly like *ch* in *church*.

Examples: *çekiç*, ' hammer '; *çocuk*, ' child '; *Çörçil*, ' Churchill '.

16. *d, t*

In English, *d* and its unvoiced equivalent *t* are produced with the tongue touching the gums behind the top teeth. In Turkish these consonants are produced with the tongue touching the top teeth, and are more distinct than their English equivalents.

Examples: *deniz*, ' sea '; *Türk*, ' Turk '.

17. *f, v*

The sounds of *f* and its voiced equivalent *v* are weaker than in English. The top front teeth lightly touch the inner side of the lower lip. Some speakers pronounce *v* as weakly as the English *w*, particularly when it occurs between *u* and *a*: *yuva*, ' nest '; *kavun*, ' melon '. *Tavuk*, ' chicken ', is often seen written *TAUK* outside food-shops, an indication of how weak the *v* is in popular speech.

18. *g, k*

(1) Before or after a back vowel (*a, ı, o, u*), *g* and *k* have the sounds heard at the beginning of English *go* and *come* respectively.

Examples: *gam*, ' grief '; *kılıbık*, ' hen-pecked husband '.

(2) Before or after a front vowel (*e, i, ö, ü*), the sounds of *g* and *k* are palatalized, that is, they are followed by a *y*-sound, like English *g* and *c* in *angular, cure*.

Examples: *göz* [g^{y}öz], ' eye '; *kürek* [k^{y}ürek^y], ' oar '.

(3) In some words of Arabic and Persian origin, g and k are also palatalized before a and u, which are then marked with a circumflex accent: â, û.

Examples: *kâtip* [kʸātip], 'secretary'; *mezkûr* [mezkʸur], 'aforementioned'; *gâvur* [gʸavur], 'infidel, Giaour'. Distinguish carefully between *kar*, 'snow', and *kâr* [kʸar], 'profit'.

(4) There is one regrettable complication: in Arabic borrowings the letters *ki*, which according to the rule stated in section (2) of this paragraph should be pronounced [kʸi], may represent [ki]: e.g., *hakikat*, 'truth'. Under the influence of the spelling, Turkish schoolchildren sometimes pronounce this word as [hakʸikat]. To avoid confusion, some writers prefer the spelling *hakıykat*.

19. ğ

(1) When at the end of a word or followed by a consonant, ğ lengthens the preceding vowel.

Examples: *dağ* [dɑː], 'mountain'; *ağda* [ɑːdɑ], 'in the net'; *iğne* [iːnɛ], 'needle'.

(2) When preceded and followed by a back vowel (*a, ı, o, u*), the preceding vowel is lengthened and the following vowel is lost or almost lost, except when one of the two vowels is *u*, when both vowels are generally pronounced distinctly and the ğ may be heard as a faint [w].

Examples: *uğur* [ʊːr], 'luck'; *dağın*, [dɑːn], 'of the mountain'; *soğuk* [sowʊk] also [soːk] and [soʊk], 'cold'.

(3) When preceded and followed by a front vowel (*e, i, ö, ü*), ğ is normally pronounced as a weak *y*-sound, as in the English *paying*.

Examples: *diğer* [dijɛr], 'other'; *eğer* [ejɛr], 'if'.

(4) In a few words, notably *dövmek*, 'to beat', and *övmek*, 'to praise', the *v* is sometimes replaced by ğ in writing but not in pronunciation.

20. h

Turkish *h* is always clearly pronounced; it is not treated like the English *h* in *hour*, *honour* or *dahlia*. There is one exception: in the common masculine name *Mehmet* the *h* is not pronounced and there is a compensatory lengthening of the preceding vowel: [mɛːmɛt].

Remember to pronounce separately each letter in the combinations *ph*, *sh* and *th*; e.g., the *ph* in *şüphe*, 'doubt', and *cephe*, 'front', is pronounced as in *slap-happy*, not as in *graph*; the *th* in *müthiş*, 'terrible', as in *pit-head*, not as in *pith*.

21. *j*

As in French *jour*, English *s* in *leisure*. Occurs only in borrowed words.

Examples: *jelâtin* (*a* short), 'gelatine'; *müjde*, 'good news'.

22. *k*

See § 18.

23. *l*

(1) In Turkish, as in English, *l* has two sounds, the 'clear *l*' of *least* (phonetic [l]) and the 'dark *l*' of *told*, *wool* [ł]. In conjunction with front vowels *l* is clear; with back vowels it is dark. The distinction comes automatically to English speakers.

Examples: (a) Clear *l*: *süslü*, 'ornate'; *çöl*, 'desert'; *geldi*, 'he came'. (b) Dark *l*: *yıl*, 'year'; *kol*, 'arm'; *pul*, 'postage-stamp'.

(2) In Arabic and other foreign borrowings, however, the clear sound of *l* can occur even in conjunction with *a* and *u*. In such cases a circumflex accent is placed over these letters: *â*, *û*. The function of this accent is the same as when it is used after *g* and *k* (§ 18); it shows that the consonant preceding the vowel so marked is followed by a *y*-sound. If we used this spelling device in English, we would write *lûrid*, *illûminate*, *allûre*, but *lunatic*. The *y*-sound in Turkish is weaker than in these English examples, but is perfectly audible. Note that the vowel marked with a circumflex may be, but is not necessarily, long (§ 12).

Examples: *şelâle* [şelʸālʸe], 'cascade'; *Lâtin* [lʸatin], 'Latin'; *malûm* [mālʸūm], 'known'.

24. *m*

Exactly as in English: *anlamadım*, 'I have not understood'.

25. *n*

Much like English *n*, to which it bears the same relation as do Turkish *d* and *t* to their English counterparts (§ 16): *niçin*, 'why?'

26. p

See § 13.

27. r

Turkish *r* is pronounced with the tip of the tongue touching the ridge of gum behind the top teeth. It is never trilled. Unlike our *r*, it is pronounced wherever it occurs in writing: compare English *car* [kɑ:] with Turkish *kar* [kɑr].

28. s

Always as in English *this*, never as in *these*.
Examples: *sıcak*, ' hot '; *ulus*, ' nation '; *masa*, ' table '.

29. ş

English *sh* in *shall*.
Examples: *şimşek*, ' lightning '; *Şeykspir*, ' Shakespeare '.

30. t

See § 16.

31. v

See § 17.

32. y

(1) Initially or after a consonant, like our *y* in *yes*.
Examples: *yağ*, ' oil '; *Asya*, ' Asia '.

(2) When preceded by a vowel in the same syllable, *y* loses most of its consonantal value and forms a diphthong.
Examples: *şey*, ' thing ' (cf. § 5); *mayn*, ' mine ' (explosive; the Turkish word is borrowed from the English, and is pronounced much the same); *boy*, ' stature '.

(3) Between vowels, *y* has a far weaker sound than otherwise: compare the English *y* in *saying* with that in *yet*.
Examples: *cumhuriyet*, ' republic '; *bahtiyar*, ' fortunate '.

(4) When *y* comes between a front vowel and a consonant, the vowel is lengthened.
Examples: *öyle* [œ:lɛ], ' thus '; *babasiyle* [bɑbɑsi:lɛ], ' with his father '.

33. z

As in English: *zafer*, ' victory '; *zelzele*, ' earthquake '.

34. THE GLOTTAL STOP

The sounds of Arabic include a glottal stop (' hamza ') and a throaty gulp (' 'ain '). These sounds, in Arabic words which have passed into Turkish, are pronounced alike as a glottal stop; the sound heard in place of the *tt* in the Cockney pronunciation of *bottle*, or before the *o* in *India Office* in the mouths of speakers careful to avoid the usual pronunciation *Indiaroffice*. The glottal stop is also heard at the end of the clipped American *No !*: the attempt to represent this abrupt closure of the breath has given rise to the spelling *Nope !*

In the new Turkish writing this sound is indicated by an apostrophe: *san'at*, ' art '. But the glottal stop does not come naturally to Turks, and consequently there is a growing tendency to omit it, both from speech and from writing: *sanat*. It is retained when its omission would cause confusion with a similar word; e.g., *telin*, ' of the wire ', but *tel'in*, ' cursing '.

35. DOUBLED CONSONANTS

Doubled consonants represent not two separate sounds but one on which the speaker dwells longer than he would on a single consonant. Compare the *p*-sound in *lamp-post*. Distinguish carefully between, e.g., *eli*, ' his hand ', and *elli*, ' fifty ', and remember that a black ace is not the same thing as a black case. See also § 45.

VOWEL HARMONY

36. The principle of vowel harmony pervades the whole of Turkish grammar, and is largely responsible for the musical quality which has caused the language to be described as ' The Italian of the East '.

For the purposes of vowel harmony, vowels are classified as back or front, high or low, rounded or unrounded (§ 3), as shown in the table below. The finer distinctions are ignored. The

	Unrounded		Rounded	
	Low	High	Low	High
Back . . .	a	ı	o	u
Front . . .	e	i	ö	ü

student will find it useful to copy the table on to a card, to avoid constantly having to turn back.

37. GENERAL LAW OF VOWEL HARMONY

If the vowel of the first syllable of a word is a back vowel, so, too, are the vowels of subsequent syllables.

If the vowel of the first syllable of a word is a front vowel, so, too, are the vowels of subsequent syllables.

Examples: (back) *çalışkan,* 'industrious'; *salıncak,* 'swing'; *dokuz,* 'nine'; *doksan,* 'ninety'; *olmadılar,* 'they did not become'.

(Front) *çekingen,* 'shy'; *gelincik,* 'poppy'; *sekiz,* 'eight'; *seksen,* 'eighty'; *ölmediler,* 'they did not die'.

Exceptions: (1) a small number of Turkish words, among the commonest being: *anne,* 'mother'; *kardeş,* 'brother'; *elma,* 'apple'; *şişman,* 'fat'; *hangi,* 'which?' and *inanmak,* 'to believe'.

(2) The six invariable suffixes *-daş, -yor, -ken, -leyin, -mtrak* and *-ki*. The last is only a partial exception, as it does change to *-kü* after *ü*.

(3) Compound words, e.g., *bugün* (*bu,* 'this', and *gün,* 'day'), 'to-day'. The word *öbür,* 'the other', is a good example of the force of vowel harmony. It was once *o bir,* 'that one', but the *o* rounded the *i* into *ü,* while the *i* turned the *o* into the front *ö*.

(4) Arabic and other foreign borrowings. Frequently there is a partial application of the principle even to these. For example, the English football term 'penalty' appears in Turkish not as *penalti* but as *penaltı,* the front *i* changing to back *ı* under the influence of the preceding back *a*. The French *épaulette* becomes *apolet.* The standard Turkish for 'bus' is *otobüs,* a phonetic spelling of the French *autobus,* but in vulgar speech the pronunciations *otobus* and even *otobos* are heard, as the front *ü* does not come naturally after the two back *o*'s. Similarly, the French *vapeur,* 'steamship', has become *vapur,* though the phonetic Turkish spelling would be *vapör*.

38. SPECIAL LAW OF VOWEL HARMONY

(1) Unrounded vowels are followed by unrounded vowels.

(2) Rounded vowels are followed by low unrounded or high rounded vowels.

39. Combining the general and the special laws, we arrive at the following:

a is followed by	*a* or	*ı*
e	,,	,,	*e* ,,	*i*
ı	,,	,,	*ı* ,,	*a*
i	,,	,,	*e* ,,	*i*
o	,,	,,	*a* ,,	*u*
ö	,,	,,	*e* ,,	*ü*
u	,,	,,	*a* ,,	*u*
ü	,,	,,	*e* ,,	*ü*

Exception: *a* may be followed by *u* if the intervening consonant is *b*, *p*, *m* or *v*; for example, *tapu*, 'title-deed'; *avuç*, 'hollow of the hand'; *abuk sabuk*, 'nonsensical'; *çamur*, 'mud'.

It will be seen that *o* and *ö* occur as a rule only in the first syllable of Turkish words.

40. VOWEL HARMONY OF SUFFIXES

It follows that the Turkish suffix, with the exceptions noted in § 37(2), has a chameleon-like quality; its vowel changes according to the vowel of the preceding syllable. For example, the suffix of the dative case, denoting 'to', is the appropriate low vowel. As *o* and *ö* do not occur in suffixes, the choice is between *a* (after back vowels) and *e* (after front vowels). Thus:

> *ev*, house; *ev-e*,* to the house
> *otobüs*, bus; *otobüs-e*, to the bus
> *orman*, forest; *orman-a*, to the forest
> *vapur*, steamer; *vapur-a*, to the steamer

We therefore say that the dative suffix is *-e/-a*. We may use instead the notation *-e²*, meaning that the suffix is one of the two low, unrounded vowels, *e* or *a*. Similarly, we may say that the suffix of the genitive case, denoting 'of', is *-in⁴*; that is, it is one of the four high vowels plus *n*: *-in*, *-ın*, *-un* or *-ün*. Thus:

> *ev-in*, of the house
> *otobüs-ün*, of the bus
> *orman-ın*, of the forest
> *vapur-un*, of the steamer

* Note that this word must be spelled *eve*. Suffixes are never hyphenated in Turkish; hyphens are used in this book only to make clearer the process of word-building.

In the absence of any note to the contrary, it may be assumed that any suffix containing an *e* is subject to the two-fold mutation, while any containing an *i* is subject to the four-fold mutation.

41. EXCEPTIONAL VOWEL HARMONY

There are a number of foreign borrowings, many of them ending in clear *l* (see § 23), whose last syllables contain an *a*, *o* or *u*, yet which take front vowels in their suffixes (although not all Turks are equally careful in this respect).

Examples: *rol*, 'rôle', *rol-ün*, 'of the rôle'; *saat*, 'hour', *saat-in*, 'of the hour'; *mahsul*, 'produce', *mahsul-ün*, 'of the produce'.

Rather than give rules for recognizing such words, it will be simpler to indicate them in the Vocabularies thus: *rol (-lü)*; *saat (-ti)*; *mahsul (-lü)*.

CHANGES IN CONSONANTS

42. Turkish words hardly ever end in the voiced consonants *b*, *c*, *d* or *g*, and when these sounds occur at the end of foreign borrowings they change to the corresponding unvoiced *p*, *ç*, *t* or *k*. Thus the Arabic for 'book', *kitāb*, becomes *kitap* in Turkish; the masculine name *Ahmad* becomes *Ahmet*. The French *garde-robe* appears as *gardrop*, 'wardrobe, cloakroom'. The Persian *rang*, 'colour', appears as *renk*. The English *bridge* (the card-game) appears as *briç*. An increasing number of writers, however, prefer the spellings *kitab*, *Ahmed*, etc., though this does not affect the pronunciation.

43. When a suffix beginning with a vowel is added to some nouns of one syllable and most nouns of more than one syllable, ending in *p*, *ç*, *t* or *k*, the final consonant changes to *b*, *c*, *d* or *ğ* respectively. Thus with the possessive suffix of the third person -i^4 (§ 40):

> *kitap*, book; *kitab-ı*, his book
> *ağaç*, tree; *ağac-ı*, his tree
> *armut*, pear; *armud-u*, his pear
> *ayak*, foot; *ayağ-ı*, his foot

Nouns whose final consonants are *not* subject to this change will be indicated in the Vocabularies thus: *renk (-gi)*, 'colour'; *et (-ti)*, 'meat'; *sepet (-ti)*, 'basket'.

This means that the *k* of *renk* becomes *g* (not *ğ*) before a suffix beginning with a vowel, while the *t* of *sepet* and of *et* remains unchanged.

The change occurs less regularly in verbs. Consequently, in the Vocabularies verbs which *are* subject to this change will be indicated, thus: *etmek* (*ed-*), ' to do '. Verbs not specially noted do not change the final consonant of their stem.

44. If a suffix beginning with *c*, *d* or *g* is added to a word ending in an unvoiced consonant (*ç, f, h, k, p, s, ş* or *t*), the initial *c*, *d* or *g* of the suffix is unvoiced, changing to *ç, t* or *k*.* For example, the suffix *-dir*⁴ means ' is ':

> *kitab-ı-dır*, it is his book; *kitap-tır*, it is the book
> *armud-u-dur*, it is his pear; *armut-tur*, it is the pear
> *sepet-i-dir*, it is his basket; *sepet-tir*, it is the basket
> *otobüs-ü-dür*, it is his bus; *otobüs-tür*, it is the bus

45. Doubled consonants at the end of Arabic borrowings are reduced to single consonants in Turkish. Thus the Arabic *haqq*, ' right ', appears as *hak*. When followed, however, by a suffix beginning with a vowel, the doubled consonant is preserved: *hakkı*, ' his right '. Such words will be shown thus: *hak* (*-kkı*).

46. Two consonants do not come together at the beginning of Turkish words, and there is a tendency in speech and writing to separate two consonants at the beginning of foreign borrowings; so for ' train ' we find *tiren* as well as *tren*, for ' club ' *kulüp* as well as *klüp*. *Şilep*, ' cargo-boat ', is the German *Schlepp*.

Sometimes instead, a vowel, usually *i*, is added before two initial consonants: *istimbot*, ' small steamboat '; *isterlin*, ' pound sterling '; *İslâv*, ' Slav '.

47. There are some twenty common words of two syllables in which the vowel of the second syllable drops out when a suffix beginning with a vowel is added: e.g., *isim*, ' name ', *ism-i*, ' his name '; *oğul*, ' son ', *oğl-u*, ' his son '. See the example *şehir* in § 63. Nouns of this type will be shown thus: *oğul* (*-ğlu*), ' son '; *şehir* (*-hri*), ' city '.

48. Arabic borrowings originally ending in the letter *'ain*

---

* This is a convenient but not strictly correct way of describing the phenomenon. It is wrong to regard the word for ' is ', for example, as an original *dir* which in certain circumstances changes to *tir, dır, tur*, etc. It is accurate, though impossibly long-winded, to say that the Turkish for ' is ' is a dental, voiced or unvoiced according to the nature of the preceding consonant, plus a high vowel, rounded or unrounded, back or front, according to the nature of the preceding vowel, plus *r*.

(§ 34) are regarded as ending as a consonant. The possessive suffix of the third person (§ 43), -*i*⁴, takes the form -*si*⁴ after vowels, e.g., *gemi-si*, ' his ship '. But ' his mosque ' is *cami-i*, ' his subject ' is *mevzu-u*, ' his square ' is *murabba-ı*, all these words originally ending in '*ain* (*cami'*, *mevzu'*, *murabba'*). Already, however, a great many people say *camisi* for ' his mosque ', and it is probable that this rule will not outlive the generation who were brought up in the time of the Arabic alphabet and remember the original spelling.

ACCENT AND STRESS

49. The problem of accent and stress in Turkish is an involved one, to give a full account of which would result in something resembling an opera-score. The simple rule is that the stress falls on the first syllable but that there is a more obvious tonic accent, i.e., a rise in the pitch of the voice, usually on the last syllable; compare the way we say ' Really? ' to express incredulity, with the stress on the first syllable but an unmistakable rise in pitch on the last. It is this rise in pitch that will be referred to as ' the accent '.

The chief exception to the rule is that place-names are hardly ever accented on the last syllable. The accented syllable of place-names and of other words not conforming to the rule will be shown thus: *Paris*; *İngiltere*, ' England '; *yalnız*, ' only '.

Unless otherwise indicated, if the accent comes on the last syllable of a word it remains at the end, even if the word is lengthened by the addition of suffixes: *ordu*, ' army '; *ordumuz*, ' our army '; *ordumuzda*, ' in our army '. But in words where the accent is on a syllable other than the last, it remains on that same syllable: *Türkiye*, ' Turkey '; *Türkiyede*, ' in Turkey '.

PUNCTUATION

50. It is usual to put a comma after the subject, especially when it comes at the beginning of a long sentence. A comma is often found where we would use a semicolon. Three dots (. . .) are used far more frequently than in English to show that a thought has not been completely expressed.

Reported speech is not always enclosed in quotation-marks, and Turkish printers seem to prefer the Continental type of arrow-head quotation-marks.

The apostrophe, in addition to representing the glottal stop (§ 34), is also used to separate names, particularly foreign names, from any grammatical endings that may be attached, to make it clear how much is name and how much is suffix. Thus: *Holivud'a*, ' to Hollywood '; *Honolulu'da*, ' in Honolulu '; *Gandhi'nin*, ' Gandhi's '; *Stalin'in*, ' Stalin's '.

The most disconcerting trick of punctuation is the use of brackets round book-titles, foreign words or words specially emphasized, where we would use inverted commas or italics: *Tank sayısı* (15.000) *i geçmiştir*, ' The number of tanks has passed *15,000* '.

LESSON ONE

51. GENDER

There is no distinction of gender in Turkish grammar. The pronoun of the third person, for example, *o* means ' he ', ' she ' or ' it ' according to the context. To save space, the alternatives will not be noted every time. When, for instance, *oldu* is given as meaning ' he became ', the reader must bear in mind that it may also mean ' she became ' or ' it became '. Similarly, *yeri*, ' his place ', may also be ' her place ' or ' its place '.

52. THE INDEFINITE ARTICLE

The indefinite article ' a ' is the same as the word for ' one ': *bir*. *Bir ev*, ' a house '; *bir göz*, ' an eye '.

53. THE PLURAL SUFFIX

The sign of the plural is *-ler/-lar* added directly to the noun before any other suffix:

> *ev*, house; *evler*, houses
> *kız*, girl; *kızlar*, girls
> *göz*, eye; *gözler*, eyes
> *elma*, apple; *elmalar*, apples

In such expressions as ' to write letters ', ' to sell newspapers ', ' to smoke cigarettes ', the plural suffix is not used, the noun in the singular denoting the class, as in ' to hunt tiger '; ' does the baby eat egg? '; not one egg or a plurality of eggs, but egg in general.

54. THE CASES

There are five case-suffixes which may be added to a Turkish noun or pronoun to show its relation to the other words in the sentence, but the student need not fear that he will have to master a vast battery of declensions such as intimidate the beginner in German or Latin. As has been briefly explained in the Introduction, the suffixes of Turkish are regular and, apart from the changes due to vowel harmony and consonant assimilation, invariable. The names of the cases familiar to students of

European languages will be used in this book, with two exceptions: instead of ' nominative ' and ' accusative ', we shall speak of the ' absolute case ' and the ' definite objective case ' (the latter abbreviated to ' def. obj.').

55. THE DEFINITE ARTICLE

There is no word in Turkish corresponding to the English ' the ', and only the context tells us whether or not to insert ' the ' in translating into English:

> *çay pahalı-dır*, tea is expensive
> *çay soğuk-tur*, the tea is cold

56. THE ABSOLUTE CASE

A distinction is, however, made when a noun is used as the direct object of a verb. When the noun is indefinite it remains in the simple form:

> *çay içtik*, we drank tea
> *bir adam gördüm*, I saw a man
> *adamlar gördüm*, I saw men

This simple form with no case-suffix, which may be either the subject or the indefinite object of a verb, we shall call the absolute case.

57. THE DEFINITE OBJECTIVE CASE

When the object of a verb is definite, i.e., when it is a proper name referring to a definite person, thing or place, or when the corresponding English word is preceded by ' the ', by a demonstrative adjective such as ' this, that, those ', or by a word denoting its possessor—' I lost *my* book '; ' She met *her* father '—so that we have no doubt about which person, place or thing is meant, it takes the def. obj. suffix *-i*[4] (§ 40):

> *çay-ı içtik*, we drank the tea
> *adam-ı gördüm*, I saw the man
> *adam-lar-ı gördüm*, I saw the men
> *Ahmed'i gördüm*, I saw Ahmet
> *İstanbul'u gördüm*, I saw Istanbul
> *göz-ü gördüm*, I saw the eye

If the noun ends in a vowel, a *y* is inserted as a buffer-letter, to keep the suffix distinct from the body of the word:

> *Ankara-y-ı gördüm*, I saw Ankara
> *kahve-y-i içtik*, we drank the coffee

58. The Genitive Case

The genitive suffix, denoting ' of ', is -*in*[4].

> *yol*, road; *yol-un*, of the road
> *gün*, day; *gün-ün*, of the day
> *Ahmed'in*, of Ahmet, Ahmet's
> *adam-lar-ın*, of the men, the men's

With words ending in a vowel, *n* is used as buffer-letter before the genitive suffix:

> *para*, money; *para-nın*, of the money
> *kedi*, cat; *kedi-nin*, of the cat
> *kuyu*, well; *kuyu-nun*, of the well
> *köprü*, bridge; *köprü-nün*, of the bridge

Note : Su, ' water ', has an irregular genitive *suyun* (not -*nun*), ' of the water '. The reason for this unique exception is that in Old Turkish the word ended in a *w*-sound and not in a vowel.

59. The Dative Case

The suffix of the dative case, denoting ' to, for ', is -*e*/-*a*. As with the def. obj. case, the buffer-letter *y* is used to separate the suffix from a word ending in a vowel.

> *İstanbul-a*, to Istanbul
> *Ankara-ya*, to Ankara
> *adam-a*, to, for the man
> *adam-lar-a*, to, for the men
> *köprü-ye*, to the bridge
> *köprü-ler-e*, to the bridges

The dative is the case of the indirect object, i.e., in ' Lend me the book ', ' Tell her the time ', ' Show him the way ', ' Give a dog a bone ', where we could insert ' to ' before ' me ', ' her ', ' him ' and ' dog ', all these words would be in the dative case in Turkish.

60. The Locative Case

This case denotes ' in, on, at ' and its suffix is -*de*/-*da* :

> *ev-de*, in the house
> *İstanbul-da*, in Istanbul
> *otobüs-ler-de*, on the buses
> *köprü-de*, on, at the bridge

61. THE ABLATIVE CASE

The suffix of the ablative case, denoting 'from, out of', is *-den/-dan*:

> *ev-den*, from the house
> *Ankara-dan*, from Ankara
> *Ahmet'ten* (§ 44), from Ahmet
> *kız-lar-dan*, from the girls

62. SUMMARY OF CASE-ENDINGS

In the following table, the bracketed letters are the buffer-letters, occurring only after words ending in a vowel:

Last vowel of word in absolute case	*e* or *i*	*ö* or *ü*	*a* or *ı*	*o* or *u*
Definite objective .	-(*y*)*i*	-(*y*)*ü*	-(*y*)*ı*	-(*y*)*u*
Genitive 'of' . .	-(*n*)*in*	-(*n*)*ün*	-(*n*)*in*	-(*n*)*un*
Dative 'to, for'. .	-(*y*)*e*		-(*y*)*a*	
Locative 'in, on, at' .	-*de*		-*da*	
Ablative 'from' .	-*den*		-*dan*	

For the circumstances in which the locative and ablative suffixes begin with *t* instead of *d*, see § 44.

63. SOME MODELS

To illustrate the sound-changes explained in the previous chapter, the various cases of five nouns are here tabulated. It must be emphasized that there is no need for the student to learn these models by heart, so long as he is acquainted with the Summary given in § 62 and the sound-changes.

	'bridge'	'dog'	'book'	'island'	'city' (§ 47)
Absolute .	köprü	köpek	kitap	ada	şehir
Definite objective	köprüyü	köpeği	kitabı	adayı	şehri
Genitive .	köprünün	köpeğin	kitabın	adanın	şehrin
Dative .	köprüye	köpeğe	kitaba	adaya	şehre
Locative .	köprüde	köpekte	kitapta	adada	şehirde
Ablative .	köprüden	köpekten	kitaptan	adadan	şehirden

64. Some loan-words with an original long vowel in the last syllable retain it when a vowel is added, but shorten it otherwise. Here for reference is a list of the commonest of such words:

> *cevap*, answer
> *hal* (*-li*), state, condition
> *hayat* (*-ti*), life
> *lüzum*, necessity
> *zaman*, time
> *mahkûm* (*u* short), condemned
> *mecruh*, wounded

So *hale*, ' to the condition ', has long *a*, while *halde*, ' in the condition ', has short *a*; *mecruhun*, ' of the wounded ', has the first *u* long; *mecruhtan*, ' from the wounded ', has short *u*.

65. WORD ORDER

(1) The subject of a sentence usually comes at the beginning, the verb at the end.

(2) A definite precedes an indefinite word: ' I to the boy an apple gave ', but ' I the apple to a boy gave '.

(3) English prepositions, ' by, of, from, for ' and so on are represented in Turkish by postpositions or suffixes, that is, by separate words or added syllables *following* the word to which they refer: ' from Ankara ', ' for me ', become ' Ankara-from ', ' me-for '.

(4) Qualifying words precede the words they qualify: ' that man ', ' that tall man ', ' that nearby standing tall man '. In such expressions as ' far from town ', ' bigger than you '; ' from town ', ' than you ' qualify ' far ' and ' bigger ', so the Turkish order is ' town-from far ', ' you-than bigger '.

(5) Expressions of time precede expressions of place, just after the subject at the beginning of a sentence. The student will find it useful to memorize the following model of a common type of Turkish sentence: ' Ahmet to-day town-in me-to a story told '.

Vocabulary 1 *

Ahmet, Ahmet (male name)	*İngiltere*, England
aldım, I took, bought	*İstanbul* or *İstanbul*, Istanbul
Ankara, Ankara (capital city of Turkey)	(formerly Constantinople)
bir, a, an	*kahve*, coffee, café
çay, tea	*kız*, girl, daughter
çocuk, child	*köprü*, bridge
dün, yesterday	*otobüs*, bus
elma, apple	*para*, money
ev, house	*şehir (-hri)*, city
gitti, he went, has gone	*tren*, train
gördüm, I saw	*Türkiye* or *Türkiye*, Turkey
içtik, we drank	*vapur*, steamer
	verdim, I gave

Exercise 1

(A) *Translate into English :* (1) köprüden; evlerin; kıza; paradan; vapurda; otobüslere. (2) Evde çay içtik. (3) Kızlar gördüm; kızları gördüm. (4) Ahmet dün Ankara'ya gitti. (5) Dün köprüde Ahmed'i gördüm. (6) Vapur, İngiltere'den Türkiye'ye gitti. (7) Otobüs İstanbul'a gitti. (8) Kızdan kahveyi aldım. (9) Vapurda bir çocuk gördüm. (10) Çocuğa bir elma verdim. (11) Elmayı bir çocuğa verdim. (12) Çocuk şehre gitti.

(B) *Translate into Turkish :* (1) In the café; from the steamer; in England; to the bridge; from a child. (2) I took the money from Ahmet yesterday in the train. (3) I gave the girls tea. (4) I gave the children the apples. (5) The steamer went from Istanbul to England. (6) I saw the girls yesterday in the bus. (7) We drank a coffee on the steamer. (8) The child went from the steamer to the train.

* This vocabulary contains all words used in Exercise 1. Subsequent exercises, however, will use words which have been given in the course of the lessons and only the most useful of which will be repeated in the vocabularies.

LESSON TWO

66. VERB ENDINGS

There are four sets of personal endings used with various parts of the Turkish verb. They are tabulated here for reference; only Type I need be learned at this stage.

	Type I	Type II	Type III	Type IV
Singular				
1st Person ' I ' .	-im	-m	*	-yim
2nd Person ' Thou '	-sin	-n	—	-sin
3rd Person ' He ' .	(-dir)	—	-sin	—
Plural				
1st Person ' We ' .	-iz	-k	*	-lim
2nd Person ' You ' .	-siniz	-niz	-in, -iniz	-siniz
3rd Person ' They ' .	-(dir)ler	-ler	-sinler	-ler

* There is no 1st Person of Type III.

67. THE VERB ' to be ': PRESENT TENSE

(1) The Type I endings form the present tense of the verb ' to be '. They are all suffixes, not independent words, and are subject to the fourfold vowel harmony, except of course for the *-ler/-lar* of the 3rd person plural.

	After *e or i*	After *a or ı*	After *ö or ü*	After *o or u*
I am . . .	-(y)im	-(y)ım	-(y)üm	-(y)um
Thou art (see *Note*)	-sin	-sın	-sün	-sun
He is . .	-dir	-dır	-dür	-dur
We are . .	-(y)iz	-(y)ız	-(y)üz	-(y)uz
You are . .	-siniz	-sınız	-sünüz	-sunuz
They are . .	-dir(ler)	dır(lar)	-dür(ler)	-dur(lar)

These endings are unaccented: *evde-yiz*, ' we are in the house '; *Türk-üm*, ' I am Turkish '. Note that after a vowel, *y* is inserted before *-im* and *-iz*.

(2) In written Turkish, *-dir(ler)* translates ' is, are ': *Ahmet*

32

evde-dir, ' A. is at home '; *çocuklar Ankara'da-dırlar*, ' the children
are in Ankara '. But in the latter example, as the plurality of
the subject is already shown by the *-lar* of *çocuklar*, it is enough to
write *çocuklar Ankara'da-dır*. We shall meet other examples of
this tendency towards economy in the use of suffixes.

(3) In the spoken language it is not necessary to use *-dir(ler)* at
all in such sentences; the juxtaposition of subject and predicate
is enough: *Ahmet evde ; çocuklar Ankarada*. In speech, *Ahmet
evdedir* means not ' A. is at home ' but ' A. must be at home '.
But in statements of permanent validity, *-dir(ler)* is used in speech
as well as in writing: *Demir ağır-dır*, ' Iron is heavy '; *Londra
İngiltere'de-dir*, ' London is in England '.

(4) It is usual for an inanimate plural subject to take a singular
verb; i.e., in Turkish, people are, things is. An animate plural
subject may also take a singular verb, if it represents a number of
people acting in a body.

Note : The ' thou ' form is used like the French *tu*, when addressing intimate friends, relations, children or animals. It is
best avoided by beginners.

68. The Verb ' to be ': Negative

The negative of ' to be ', with certain exceptions to be noted
later, is expressed by the word *değil*, ' not ', with the Type I
endings :

değilim, I am not   *değiliz*, we are not
değilsin, thou art not   *değilsiniz*, you are not
değil(dir), he is not   *değil(dirler)*, they are not

With the omission of *-dir* (§ 67 (3)), ' they are not ' may be
değiller.

değil also translates ' not ' without a verb: *Ahmet değil Orhan
gitti* (' Ahmet not, Orhan went '). ' It wasn't A., it was O. who
went '.

69. The indefinite article *bir* is less frequent than its English
equivalent; for example, it is not necessary to use it in negative
sentences: *çocuk değil*, ' he is not (a) child ', or with nouns denoting
one's occupation, station in life or nationality: *İngiliz-im*, ' I am
(an) Englishman '; *asker-siniz*, ' you are (a) soldier '. The reason
is that *bir* really means ' one '; if he is not of the class ' child ', it
is superfluous to say that he is not one single member of that
class. So, too, I cannot be more than one Englishman; you are

B

obviously not more than one soldier. Compare the French *vous êtes soldat.*

70. PERSONAL PRONOUNS

ben, I		*biz*, we	
sen, thou		*siz*, you	
o, he, she, it		*onlar*, they	

As verb-endings change according to the person, these forms are used mainly for emphasis: *ben tembel değilim, siz tembelsiniz,* '*I*'m not lazy, *you* are lazy'.

Of these pronouns, only *siz* is quite regular. The others show certain irregularities, which are printed in capital letters in the following table:

I	*ben*	thou	*sen*	he, she, it	*o*
me	*beni*	thee	*seni*	him, etc.	*oNu*
of me	*beniM*	of thee	*senin*	of him, etc.	*onun*
to me	*bAnA*	to thee	*sAnA*	to him, etc.	*oNa*
in me	*bende*	in thee	*sende*	in him, etc.	*oNda*
from me	*benden*	from thee	*senden*	from him, etc.	*oNdan*
we	*biz*	you	*siz*	they	*oNlar*
us	*bizi*	you	*sizi*	them	*oNları*
of us	*biziM*	of you	*sizin*	of them	*oNların*
to us	*bize*	to you	*size*	to them	*oNlara*
in us	*bizde*	in you	*sizde*	in them	*oNlarda*
from us	*bizden*	from you	*sizden*	from them	*oNlardan*

It will be seen that 'he' has an *n* before the case-suffixes and before the *-lar* of the plural. This *n* turns up in the declension of other pronouns, and is referred to as the 'pronominal *n*'.

'I' and 'we' have an *m* instead of the usual *n* in the genitive case.

'I' and 'thou' shift from the front- to the back-vowel class in the dative.

siz means 'you', singular and plural (§ 67, *Note*), and *biz,* 'we', is sometimes colloquially used for 'I'. When more than one person is referred to, these words may take the plural suffix: *bizler*, 'we'; *sizler*, 'you'.

71. POSSESSIVE SUFFIXES

Possession or relationship—'my friend, their work, its development'—is indicated by the following suffixes, which have slightly different forms according to whether they follow a vowel or a consonant. Note the unusual buffer-letter *s* of the 3rd-person-singular suffix.

		After consonants	After vowels
my . . .		-*im*⁴	-*m*
thy . . .		-*in*⁴	-*n*
his . . .		-*i*⁴	-*si*⁴
our . . .		-*imiz*⁴	-*miz*⁴
your . . .		-*iniz*⁴	-*niz*⁴
their . . .		-*leri*/-*ları*	-*leri*/*ları*

Examples:

göz-üm, my eye	*baba-m*, my father
kız-ın, thy daughter	*anne-n*, thy mother
kol-u, her arm	*para-sı*, his money
otomobil-imiz, our car	*ordu-muz*, our army
çocuklar-ınız, your children	*oda-nız*, your room
dükkân-ları, their shop	*kedi-leri*, their cat

Case-endings follow these suffixes: *gözüm-de*, 'in my eye'; *ordumuz-a*, 'to our army'; *çocuklarınız-dan*, 'from your children'. An *n* (§ 70: 'pronominal *n*') is inserted before any case endings that may be attached to the 'his' and 'their' suffixes: *kol-u-n-a*, 'to her arm'; *para-sı-n-dan*, 'from his money'; *dükkân-ları-n-da*, 'in their shop'; *kedi-leri-n-in*, 'of their cat'.

evleri can mean 'his houses' (*evler-i*) or 'their house' (*ev-leri*). Further, when -*leri*, 'their', is added to a plural noun, one *ler* drops out. So *evleri* can also mean 'their houses'.

Except in the absolute case, there is no distinction of spelling or pronunciation between the 'thy' suffix and the 'his' suffix following a consonant: *ev-in-e*, 'to thy house'; *ev-i-n-e*, 'to his house'. *kardeş-in-in*, 'of thy brother'; *kardeş-i-n-in*, 'of her brother'. For the way in which these ambiguities are avoided, see § 72 (3), (5).

Note: *su*, 'water', takes the form *suy*- before suffixes beginning with a vowel (cf. § 58, *Note*): *suyu*, 'its water', *suyunuz*, 'your water', but *suları*, 'its waters, their water(s)'.

72. THE USE OF THE POSSESSIVE SUFFIXES

(1) The function of the endings described in the previous paragraph is to show that the person or thing represented by the

word to which they are attached belongs to or is connected with some other person or thing: *oda-sı*, ' his room '; *kapı-sı*, ' its door ', *yanlış-ım*, ' my mistake '; *akıl-ları*, ' their intelligence '.

(2) If the possessor is expressed by a definite noun (§ 57)—' the Director's room, the door of my house '—the possessing noun takes the genitive ending *-in*[4] and precedes the possessed noun (cf. § 65 (4)): *Müdür-ün odası; ev-im-in kapısı* (' of-the-Director his-room '; ' of-my-house its-door '). This construction will be referred to as the Possessive Relationship.

(3) The genitive case of a personal pronoun may be used similarly, either to avoid ambiguity or for emphasis: *benim ev-im*, ' *my* house '; *onun evinde*, ' in his house '; *senin evinde*, ' in thy house '.

(4) But if the possessor is not definite, it remains in the absolute form: *misafir odası*, ' guest-room ' (which does not belong to any specific guest); *ev kapısı*, ' house-door '. This construction will be referred to as the Qualifying Relationship.

(5) In such a phrase as ' the girls' room ', theoretically ' of-the-girls their-room ', *kızlar-ın oda-ları*, the plurality of the possessor is already shown by the *lar* of *kızların*, so instead we find *kızların oda-sı* (' . . . her-room '). Cf. § 67 (2). ' The girls' rooms ', however, must be *kızların odaları*.

(6) In the colloquial, the genitive forms of the pronouns of the first and second persons may be used *instead* of the possessive suffixes: *benim oda* (' of-me the room '), ' my room '; *bizim köy*, ' our village '; *senin ev*, ' thy house '; *sizin sokak*, ' your street '. The literary forms would be *(benim) odam, (bizim) köyümüz, (senin) evin, (sizin) sokağınız* (§ 43).

The 3rd-person suffix, however, cannot be omitted: *(onun) odası*, ' his room '; *sokakları* or *onların sokağı* (see (5) above), ' their street '.

Note : ' own ' is *kendi : kendi evim*, ' my own house '; *kendi odanız*, ' your own room '.

73. THE INTERROGATIVE PARTICLE

(1) To turn any word into a question, we put *mi*[4] after it. The main accent in the sentence (except as shown in § 83 (1)) falls on the syllable before the *mi*, which itself is never accented. Consider the following sentences:

> *Bakan İngiltere-ye gitti.* The Minister has gone to England.
> *Bakan İngiltereye gitti mi?* Has the M. gone to England?

Bakan İngiltereye mi gitti? Has the M. gone to *England?*
Bakan mı İngiltereye gitti? Has the *Minister* gone to England?

(2) In interrogative sentences consisting of an adjective or noun and part of the verb 'to be', such as 'Are you tired?' 'Is her husband English?' it is the tiredness or Englishness that is in question, not the person's existence, so the *mi* follows the adjective or noun, not the 'is' or 'are': *Yorgun mu-sunuz? Kocası İngiliz mi-dir?*

(3) *değil mi?* ('Not?') is used like the French *n'est ce pas?* to seek confirmation of a statement.

Vapur-u gördük, değil mi? We saw the steamer, didn't we?
Güzel, değil mi? Pretty, isn't she?
Ankaraya gitti, değil mi? He's gone to Ankara, hasn't he?

Note: The word *müdür* may be either the noun meaning 'director, administrator' or the interrogative particle plus 'is' when following an *ö* or *ü*: *Müdür Türk müdür?* 'Is the Director a Turk?' In practice there is no likelihood of confusion, especially in conversation, as 'director', like most nouns, is accented on the last syllable, whereas neither *mi*[4] nor *dir*[4] are ever accented.

74. ADJECTIVES

(1) Turkish adjectives are often used as nouns: *genç çocuklar*, 'young children'; *bir genç*, 'a young person, youth'; *gençler*, 'the young'. *Hasta*, 'ill'; *bir hasta*, 'a sick person, a patient'.

(2) Where English has the indefinite article plus adjective plus noun: 'a big house, an intelligent girl', Turkish as a rule says 'big a house; intelligent a girl': *büyük bir ev, zeki bir kız*, less commonly *bir büyük ev, bir zeki kız*.

(3) The attributive adjective always precedes its noun, as in English ('black cat') and never follows it as in French (*chat noir*).

Vocabulary 2

adam, man
akşam, evening
arkadaş, friend
baba, father
bu, this
çalışkan, industrious
dükkân, shop

eski, old (of things), former (of people)
evet, yes
Galata, Galata (business quarter of Istanbul)
hayır, no
istasyon, railway-station

iş, work, job, matter, business	*pek*, very
karakol, police-station	*sigara*, cigarette
kitap, book	*sinema*, cinema
komşu, neighbour	*sonra*, after(wards)
kutu, box	*şimdi*, now
meşgul (-lü), busy	*uzak*, far
mühim, important	*yakın* (with dative), near (to)
otomobil, motor-car	*yeni*, new

Exercise 2

(A) *Translate into English :* (1) Baba-nız istasyon-a gitti mi?
(2) Arkadaş-ımız-ın dükkân-ı Galata'da, karakol-a yakın. (3)
Onu otobüs-te değil, tren-de gördüm. (4) Sizin kutu-nuz-dan
değil, kendi kutu-m-dan bir sigara aldım. (5) Bu kitab-ı
arkadaş-ınız Ahmet'ten aldım. (6) Bu adam-ın ev-i istasyondan
uzak değil, pek yakın-dır. (7) O, dün akşam sinema-ya gitti,
sonra biz arkadaşlar-ımız-ın evinde kahve içtik. (8) Yeni müdür
çalışkan mı-dır?—Hayır, pek çalışkan değildir. (9) Ev-leri
Galata'da, değil mi?—Evet, köprü-ye yakın. (10) Kutu-yu bu
adam-a verdim, değil mi? (11) Çocuk, odasındadır. Çocuğun
odasındadır. (12) Komşuların evleri. Komşuların evi.

(B) *Translate into Turkish :* (1) I bought this car from your
father. It's not very old. (2) The former Director went to
Ankara yesterday evening, didn't he? (3) My daughter has
gone to our friend's shop. (4) The police-station is not far from
our house. (5) This is not your money. (6) I saw the Director's
daughter on the steamer this evening. (7) Your box is now on
the train. (8) Her job isn't very important. (9) Your friend's
father is a very industrious man, isn't he? (10) Are you busy
now?—Yes, I'm very busy.

LESSON THREE

75. QUALIFYING NOUNS

(1) In English we can make one noun qualify another simply by putting the two nouns side by side: ' hand-bag, pigskin, bombing-plane '. The Turkish practice is to put the two words in the Qualifying Relationship (§ 72 (4)) and say ' hand its-bag, pig its-skin, bombing its-plane ': *el çanta-sı, domuz deri-si, bombardıman uçağı (uçak,* ' aeroplane '). *-(s)i* is the hardest-worked suffix in the language, and its uses must be understood. Study carefully the following examples:

Çarşamba gün-ü	(Wednesday its-day)	Wednesday
1953 sene-si	(1953 its-year)	the year 1953
Nisan ay-ı	(April its-month)	the month of April
kılıç balığ-ı	(sword its-fish)	sword-fish
elma ağac-ı	(apple its-tree)	apple-tree
çilek dondurma-sı	(strawberry its-ice)	strawberry-ice
yatak oda-sı	(bed its-room)	bedroom
telefon rehber-i	(telephone its-guide)	telephone-directory
kahve fincan-ı	(coffee its-cup)	coffee-cup
harp zengin-i	(war its-rich)	war-profiteer
Kıbrıs ada-sı	(Cyprus its-island)	the island of Cyprus
İstanbul belediye-si	(I. its-municipality)	the municipality of I.
Atlantik pakt-ı	(Atlantic its-pact)	the Atlantic Pact.

(2) The plurals of such compounds are formed by inserting *-ler* before the possessive suffix: *elma ağaçları,* ' apple-trees '; *harp zenginleri,* ' war-profiteers '; *yatak odaları,* ' bedrooms '.

(3) The ' its ' suffix is dropped if a possessive suffix is used to denote the possessor: *yatak oda-m,* ' my bedroom '; *yatak odanız,* ' your bedroom '. It follows that *yatak odası* may mean ' his bedroom ' as well as ' bedroom '; in the former event the device noted in § 72 (3) is employed: *onun yatak odası.*

(4) There are a few expressions which are written and treated as single words, although they were originally compounds of this

kind. The two preceding sections of this paragraph do not apply to them. The commonest are:

Binbaşı	(thousand its-head)	Major
Yüzbaşı	(hundred its-head)	Captain
Onbaşı	(ten its-head)	Corporal
ayakkabı	(foot its-cover)	footwear, shoes
denizaltı	(see § 78)	submarine

Examples: *Binbaşılar,* 'Majors'; *Yüzbaşıya,* 'to the Captain'; *çocuğun ayakkabısı,* 'the child's shoes'; *denizaltıda,* 'in the submarine'.

Note : Place-names consisting of two words in the Qualifying Relationship tend to lose the possessive *-(s)i*: *Topkapı* was once *Top-kapı-sı* ('gun its-gate'); *Erenköyü* is fast becoming *Erenköy,* so for 'at E.' one may hear *Erenköyünde* or *Erenköyde.*

76. It will be recalled that, when a noun represents the definite possessor of anything, it takes the genitive suffix (§ 72 (2)); *domuz derisi,* 'pigskin', but *domuzun derisi,* 'the skin of the (specific) pig'; *kuyu suy-u,* 'well-water', but *bu kuyunun suyu,* 'the water of this well'; *otomobil tekerlek-leri,* 'car-wheels', but *otomobilin tekerlekleri,* 'the wheels of the car'. Nevertheless, place-names are generally left in the absolute form as qualifiers, like the first elements in the examples in § 75, even when they might be regarded as possessing the following noun: *İstanbul halk-ı,* 'the people of I.'; *Ankara sinemalarında,* 'in the cinemas of A.'; *Türkiye Başbakan-ı,* 'the Prime Minister of Turkey'. The use of the genitive case is, however, obligatory if the place-name is separated by another word from the noun it qualifies: *İstanbul hayat-ı,* 'Istanbul life', but *İstanbul'un sanat hayat-ı,* 'the artistic life of Istanbul'; *Semerkant çini-leri,* 'Samarkand porcelains', but *Semerkand'ın mavi çini-leri,* 'the blue porcelains of Samarkand'.

77. Where we use an adjective of nationality—'English history, the Turkish Army, French literature'—Turkish uses a qualifying noun, generally identical with the noun denoting a person of the nationality concerned: *İngiliz tarih-i* ('Englishman his-history'), *Türk ordusu* ('Turk his-army'), *Fransız edebiyat-ı* ('Frenchman his-literature').

Sometimes, however, there are two different nouns, e.g., *bir Amerikalı,* 'an American', but *Amerikan ordusu,* 'the A. Army'.

78. Compound Nouns

The marks of a compound noun are that the elements composing it are written as one word and do not both retain their primary meaning.

Examples:

> *bu*, this; *gün*, day: *bugün*, to-day
> *deniz*, sea; *alt-ı,* its-underside: *denizaltı*, submarine
> *hanım*, lady; *el-i*, her-hand: *hanımeli*, honey-suckle
> *baş*, head; *bakan*, minister: *başbakan*, Prime Minister
> *kara*, black; *yel*, wind: *karayel*, North-west wind
> *dedi*, he said; *kodu*, he put: *dedikodu*, gossip (noun)

Note that compound nouns not containing a verb are accented on the last syllable of their first element.

79. The Verb: Infinitive

The infinitive of the English verb is the form 'to see, to go, to want', etc. The Turkish equivalent ends in *-mek/-mak*: *görmek*, 'to see'; *gitmek*, 'to go'; *anlamak*, 'to understand'; *bulmak*, 'to find'. That portion of each infinitive to which the *-mek/-mak* is added (*gör-*, *git-*, *anla-*, *bul-*) is known as the stem.

The infinitive is a noun, and may be the subject or object of a verb: '*to run away* seems cowardly'; 'I want *to sing*'.

80. List of Essential Verbs

açmak, to open
almak, to take, buy, receive *
anlamak, to understand
aramak, to seek
atmak, to throw
bakmak, to look (with dative: 'at, after')
başlamak, to begin (with dative)
beğenmek, to like, approve of
beklemek, to wait, await, expect
bırakmak, to leave
bilmek, to know, guess
bulmak, to find
çalişmak, to work, strive

çekmek, to pull
çıkmak, to go out, go up
demek, to say
dinlemek, to listen, listen to
durmak, to stand, stop
duymak, to feel, hear
düşmek, to fall
düşünmek, to think (about)
etmek (*ed-* § 43), to do
geçmek, to pass
gelmek, to come
getirmek, to bring
girmek, to enter (with dative)
gitmek (*gid-*), to go

* In case of ambiguity, *satın almak* ('to take by sale') is used for 'to buy'.

göndermek, to send
görmek, to see
hatırlamak, to remember
içmek, to drink, smoke
istemek, to want, ask for
işitmek, to hear
kalmak, to remain, be left
kalkmak, to rise, be removed, start (train, etc.)
kapamak, to shut
kaybetmek (-ed-), to lose
kırmak, to break
komak, koymak, to put, place
konuşmak, to speak, discuss
koşmak, to run
kullanmak, to use
okumak, to read
olmak, to be, become, occur
oturmak, to sit, live (dwell)
öğrenmek, to learn
ölmek, to die
sanmak, to think, suppose

satmak, to sell
saymak, to count, esteem
seçmek, to choose
sevmek, to love, like
sormak, to ask, ask about
söylemek, to say, tell
tanımak, to know, recognize
taşımak, to carry
tutmak, to hold
uçmak, to fly
unutmak, to forget
uyanmak, to awake
uyumak, to sleep
vermek, to give
vurmak, to strike
yapmak, to make, do
yaşamak, to live (be alive)
yatmak, to lie down, go to bed
yazmak, to write
yemek, to eat
yollamak, to send
yürümek, to walk

81. THE VERB: PAST TENSE

The various tenses of the verb are formed by adding to the stem a tense-suffix, the resulting word (the 'tense-base') being the 3rd person singular of the tense, to which personal endings are added to form the remaining persons (§ 66). The suffix of the past tense is -di[4] and with it are used the Type II endings.

iste-di-m, I wanted, have wanted
iste-di-n, thou didst want
iste-di, he wanted

iste-di-k, we wanted
iste-di-niz, you wanted
iste-di-ler, they wanted

So from:

> görmek, to see: gördüm, gördün, gördü, gördük, gördünüz, gördüler, I saw, have seen, etc.
>
> bakmak, to look (§ 44): baktım, baktın, baktı, baktık, baktınız, baktılar, I looked, have looked, etc.
>
> bulmak, to find: buldum, buldun, buldu, bulduk, buldunuz, buldular, I found, have found, etc.

82. The Verb ' to be ': Past Tense

(1) Under the English verb ' to be ' are included a number of words of different origins (be, am, is, are, was) and the same is true in Turkish. We have already met the present tense (§ 67). For the infinitive, *olmak* is used, which properly means ' to come to be, become, occur, mature '. The past tense is based on a stem *i-*, to which are added the past suffixes shown in § 81 :

idim, I was	*idik*, we were
idin, thou wert	*idiniz*, you were
idi, he was	*idiler*, they were

These forms, which are unaccented, are used either as independent words or, especially in conversation, as suffixes. In the latter case, the first *i* disappears after consonants and changes to *v* after vowels, the remainder of the word undergoing the fourfold vowel harmony.

adam idi or *adamdı*, it was the man
müdür idiniz or *müdürdünüz*, you were the director
kitap idi or *kitaptı* (§ 44), it was the book
yorgun idik or *yorgunduk*, we were tired
sinemada idiniz or *sinemadaydınız*, you were at the cinema.

(2) The interrogative *mi⁴* usually combines with *idim*, etc.:

hazır mıydım (for *mı idim*), was I ready?
hazır mıydın, wert thou ready?
hazır mıydı, was he ready?
    etc.
meşgul müydüm (for *mü idim*), was I busy?
yorgun muydum (for *mu idim*), was I tired?
tembel miydim (for *mi idim*), was I lazy?

Note : The past tense of *olmak*, ' to become ', is regular: *oldum, oldun, oldu,* etc. So *asker olmak* means ' to be *or* to become a soldier ', but *asker idim* (*askerdim*), ' I was a soldier '; *asker oldum,* ' I became a soldier '.

83. The Verb: Negative

(1) The negative of all verbs, except for those parts of ' to be ' which are based on the stem *i-*, is made by adding *me/ma* to the stem. To the negative stem so formed are added tense- and

other suffixes. The main accent in the sentence comes on the syllable before the *me/ma*.

> *istemek*, to want; *istedim*, I wanted
> *istememek*, not to want; *istemedim*, I did not want
> *bakmak*, to look; *baktınız*, you looked
> *bakmamak*, not to look; *bakmadınız*, you did not look
> *olmak*, to become; *oldum*, I became
> *olmamak*, not to become; *olmadım*, I did not become

(2) The past tense of *olmamak* when it means 'not to be', in other words, the negative of *idim* (§ 82) is:

> *değil idim* or *değildim*, I was not
> *değil idin* or *değildin*, thou wert not
> *değil idi* or *değildi*, he was not
> *değil idik* or *değildik*, we were not
> *değil idiniz* or *değildiniz*, you were not
> *değil idiler* or *değildiler* or *değillerdi*, they were not

(3) The negative interrogative is formed as explained in §§ 73, 82 (2): *Bakmadınız mı?* 'Didn't you look?' *Olmadım mı?* 'Didn't I become?' *Hazır değil miydik?* 'Weren't we ready?'

84. 'To Have'—*Var, Yok*

The words *var* and *yok* ('existent' and 'non-existent') are used for 'there is' and 'there is not' respectively: *Bu şehirde iyi bir otel var mı?* 'Is there a good hotel in this city?' *Odamda su yok*, 'There's no water in my room'. These two words are employed where English uses the verb 'to have', thus: *Bir kardeş-im var (dır)* ('a my-brother existent is'), 'I have a brother'; *iş-iniz yok mu?* ('your-work non-existent?'), 'Have you no work?' Answer: *var*, 'I have', or *yok*, 'I have not'. *Para-m yok*, 'I have no money'. An alternative translation for this is *ben-de para yok* ('in-me money non-existent'). The latter does not denote such absolute penury as *param yok*, but means rather 'I've no money on me'.

Past tense: *müdür-ün otomobil-i yok-tu* ('the director's car was-non-existent'), 'the director had no car'; *bir komşu-muz var-dı*, 'we had a neighbour'.

var, yok are used only in the present tense and with those parts of *olmak* based on the stem *i-* (see § 183). Otherwise the requisite part of *olmak* is used alone: 'we shall have a holiday' becomes 'an our-holiday will be'.

Note : Distinguish between *vardı* (§ 82), 'there was ', and *vardı*, ' he arrived ', past tense of *varmak*.

85. The object of a verb is often not expressed when it is quite clear from the context: ' He showed me the coat, but I didn't like (it) so I didn't buy (it) '. Numerous examples will be found in the Exercises.

86. THE SUFFIX -*li*

(1) The addition of -*li*[4] to a noun makes an adjective or noun meaning ' characterized by or possessing whatever the original noun represents '. The resemblance to the English suffix -*ly*, as in *shapely* from *shape*, is a useful aid to the memory, but is sheer coincidence.

> *Bizans*, Byzantium; *Bizanslı*, Byzantine
> *Londra*, London; *Londralı*, Londoner
> *kıymet*, value; *kıymetli*, valuable
> *uzun boy*, long stature; *uzun boylu*, tall
> *orta*, middle; *orta boylu*, of medium height
> *mâna*, meaning; *mânalı*, significant
> *rutubet*, moisture; *rutubetli*, moist, damp
> *ev*, house, home; *evli*, married
> *köy*, village; *köylü*, villager
> *sen*, thou, *ben*, I; *senli benli*, informally (cf. § 67, *Note*)
> *resim* (-*smi*), picture; *resimli*, illustrated

(2) -*li* is also added to adjectives of colour, thus: *kırmızı*, ' red '; *kırmızılı*, ' dressed in red '.

(3) If -*li* is added to a phrase containing a qualifying noun the possessive suffix is dropped: *Osman ad-ı* (' Osman its-name '), ' the name " Osman " ' '; *Osman ad-lı bir genç*, ' a young man named O.' (' O.-named '); *23 Nisan tarih-i* (' 23 April its-date '), ' the date 23 April '; *23 Nisan tarih-li mektub-unuz*, ' your letter dated 23 April '.

87. THE SUFFIX -*siz*

-*siz* means ' without ':

> *akıl*, intelligence; *akılsız*, stupid
> *son*, end; *sonsuz*, endless
> *fayda*, use; *faydasız*, useless
> *edep*, good breeding; *edepsiz*, ill-bred, mannerless
> *sen*, thou; *sensiz*, without thee
> *o*, he; *o-n-suz* (§ 70), without him

So *kıymetsiz*, ' valueless '; *mânasız*, ' meaningless '.

Vocabulary 3

ada, island
adres, address
ağaç, tree
ana, *anne*,* mother
asıl, *gerçek*, real, genuine
bahçe, garden
başka, other, different
başlıca, chief, principal
belki, perhaps
bile (follows the word it modifies), even
boş, empty, vacant
büyük, great, big
cumhūriyet (*-ti*), republic
çok, many, much, a lot of
devlet (*-ti*), State
efendi, master
eser, work, effect
fakat, but
Fâtih, Conqueror (Sultan Mehmet II)
halk (*-kı*), people, the common people
ıçki, alcoholic drink
inhisar, monopoly
iskele, quay, landing-stage
kapalı, closed, covered

kardeş, brother *or* sister; *kız-kardeş*, sister
kaynak, source, spring
kazanç, profit, gain
kılık, aspect, costume, ' get-up '
maalesef, unfortunately
memleket (*-ti*), country, land
mēmur, official, Civil Servant
meyva, fruit
niçin, why?
oda, room
oğul (*-ğlu*), son
otel, hotel
palto, overcoat
pasaport (*-tu*), passport
perîşan, untidy, disordered
polis, police, policeman
saat (*-ti*), hour, watch, clock
sabah, morning
sarı, yellow
sene, *yıl*, year
sergi, exhibition, display
sokak, street
şapka, hat
taşınmak, to move (house)
vakit (*-kti*), time
yatak, bed

Exercise 3

(A) *Translate into English :* (1) İstanbul sergi-si-ne gitmek istedik, fakat vakt-imiz yoktu. (2) Polis memurları pasaport-um-a bakmadılar bile. (3) Arkadaşlar-ınız dün başka bir ev-e taşındılar, değil mi? (4) Bu sabah Adalar iskele-si-nde siz-i bir saat bekledik; niçin gelmediniz? (5) Sigara almak istedi fakat dükkân kapalı-ydı.—Başka bir dükkân yok mu-ydu? (6) Bahçe-miz-de bir elma ağac-ı var, fakat bu yıl meyva vermedi. (7)

---

* *anne* is used only in Istanbul Turkish, and then only in the literal sense; in provincial dialects and in metaphorical uses *ana* is used: *anahat*, ' main line '; *anayol*, ' main road '.

Kardeş-iniz-ı sokak-ta perişan bir kılık-ta, palto-suz şapka-sız gördüm. (8) Yatak oda-m pek rutubetli-dir. Otel-iniz-de boş bir oda var mı?—Maalesef yok. (9) Uzun boylu çocuk müdürün oğl-u mudur?—Hayır, onun bir kız-ı var, oğlu yok. (10) Fâtih, 1453 sene-sinde (yıl-ında) İstanbul-u Bizans-lı-lar-dan aldı. (11) İçkiler inhisar-ı Cumhuriyet-in büyük bir eser-i, devlet-in başlıca bir kazanç kaynağ-ı idi. (12) (Bizim Köy) ad-lı kitab-ı oku-ma-dınız mı?

(B) *Translate into Turkish :* (1) Is your sister married? (2) He wanted to go to another hotel. (3) Is this cigarette-box new?—Yes, my mother gave it to me. (4) Perhaps he found our address in the telephone-directory. (5) Our apple-trees have given a lot of fruit this year, haven't they? (6) The girl in yellow is Orhan's sister. (7) We waited for her at the station but she didn't come. (8) My sister wanted to buy their house, but I didn't like it, it's very damp. (9) Have you left your passport at the hotel? (10) The people is the real master of the country.

LESSON FOUR

88. The Verb: Present and Present-past Tenses

The suffix of the present is -*yor*, preceded by a high vowel (§ 36), *i, ı, u or ü*, according to the nature of the preceding vowel:

> *gelmek*, to come; *geliyor*, he is coming (*or* comes at this moment)
>
> *almak*, to take; *alıyor*, he is taking
>
> *bulmak*, to find; *buluyor*, he is finding
>
> *görmek*, to see; *görüyor*, he is seeing

If the stem already ends in a high vowel, the -*yor* is added directly to it:

> *taşı-mak*, to carry; *taşı-yor*, he is carrying
>
> *koru-mak*, to protect; *koru-yor*, he is protecting

If the stem ends in a low vowel, this becomes the corresponding high vowel (see *Note*):

> *de-mek*, to say; *di-yor*, he is saying
>
> *anla-mak*, to understand; *anlı-yor*, he understands
>
> *söyle-mek*, to tell; *söylü-yor*, he is telling
>
> *kolla-mak*, to observe; *kollu-yor*, he is observing

To the present base so formed are added the present or past of the verb ' to be ' (§§ 67, 82) but not *dir*; the present base itself denotes the 3rd person singular. Consider the following:

> *Ahmet yorgun*, Ahmet is tired; *Ahmet geliyor*, A. is coming
>
> *(Ben) yorgun-um*, I am tired; *(Ben) geliyor-um*, I am coming
>
> *(Ben) yorgun-dum*, I was tired; *(Ben) geliyor-dum*, I was coming

Here are the present and present-past tenses of *gelmek*. Note the accentuation.

geliyorum, I am coming	*geliyordum,* I was coming
geliyorsun, thou art coming	*geliyordun*, thou wert coming
geliyor, he is coming	*geliyordu*, he was coming
geliyoruz, we are coming	*geliyorduk*, we were coming
geliyorsunuz, you are coming	*geliyordunuz*, you were coming
geliyorlar, they are coming	*geliyorlardı* or *geliyordular*, they were coming

As *-yor* is invariable (§ 37 (2)), these endings are the same for all verbs.

Note : These sound-changes are instances of the following rule (which like other rules is not universally obeyed) : If a suffix beginning with *y* is added to a stem ending in *e* or *a*, the *e* or *a* becomes *i* or *ı* respectively, unless both the vowel preceding the *e* or *a* and the vowel following the *y* are rounded, when the *e* or *a* becomes *ü* or *u*.

89. THE PRESENT AND PRESENT-PAST TENSES : NEGATIVE

The endings given in the preceding paragraph may be added to the negative verb-stem, the final *e* or *a* of which is then subject to the changes described above :

> *al-ma-mak*, not to take; *almıyor*, he is not taking
> *gör-me-mek*, not to see; *görmüyor*, he is not seeing
> *taşı-ma-mak*, not to carry; *taşımıyor*, he is not carrying
> *de-me-mek*, not to say; *demiyor*, he is not saying
> *anla-ma-mak*, not to understand; *anlamıyor*, he does not understand
> *söyle-me-mek*, not to tell; *söylemiyor*, he is not telling

almıyorsunuz, ' you are not taking '; *almıyordunuz*, ' you were not taking '; *görmüyorduk*, ' we were not seeing '; *söylemiyorum*, ' I am not telling ', etc.

90. THE PRESENT AND PRESENT-PAST TENSES : INTERROGATIVE

The interrogative particle *mi*[4] is placed after the present-base, except in the 3rd person plural of the present, when it follows the *lar* :

> *geliyor muyum*, am I coming? ; *gelmiyor muyum*, am I not coming?
> *geliyor musun*, art thou coming?; *gelmiyor musun*, art thou not coming?
> *geliyorlar mı*, are they coming?; *gelmiyorlar mı*, are they not coming?
> *geliyor muydum*, was I coming?; *gelmiyor muydum*, was I not coming?
> *geliyor muydunuz*, were you coming?; *gelmiyor muydunuz*, were you not coming?

91. NUMERALS: CARDINAL

bir, one	*on iki*, twelve	*otuz*, thirty
iki, two	*on üç*, thirteen	*kırk*, forty
üç, three	*on dört*, fourteen	*elli*, fifty
dört, four	*on beş*, fifteen	*altmış*, sixty
beş, five	*on altı*, sixteen	*yetmiş*, seventy
altı, six	*on yedi*, seventeen	*seksen*, eighty
yedi, seven	*on sekiz*, eighteen	*doksan*, ninety
sekiz, eight	*on dokuz*, nineteen	*yüz*, hundred
dokuz, nine	*yirmi*, twenty	*bin*, thousand
on, ten	*yirmi bir*, twenty-one	*milyon*, million
on bir, eleven	*yirmi iki*, twenty-two	*sıfır*, zero

(1) These numbers are compounded as in English, except that ' and ' is not used: *yüz otuz*, ' a hundred (and) thirty '; *bin elli*, ' a thousand (and) fifty '.

In the numbers from eleven to nineteen, the accent is on the *on*. In compound numbers above twenty, it is the last syllable of the units figure which is accented: *yirmi sekiz*, ' twenty-eight '; *otuz altı*, ' thirty-six '; *elli bir*, ' fifty-one '.

dört yüz otuz iki, ' 432 '; *bin on üç*, ' 1013 '; *bin dokuz yüz elli üç*, ' 1953 '; *yedi milyon yedi yüz yetmiş yedi bin yedi yüz yetmiş yedi*, ' 7.777.777 ' (Turks put a full stop after the thousands where we put a comma).

(2) Words preceded by a number do not normally take the plural suffix, as the use of a number greater than one necessarily implies plurality: *otuz beş yıl*, ' thirty-five years '; *iki çocuk*, ' two children '; *yedi ada*, ' seven islands '; *üç ay*, ' three months '. So with *kaç*, ' how many? '; *kaç çocuk*, ' how many children? '

The exceptions to this rule consist in a few expressions relating to well-known things: *yedi adalar*, ' the Seven (Ionian) Islands '; *üç aylar*, ' the Three (Sacred) Months (of the Islamic year) '.

(3) Certain words, the commonest being *tane* (' grain '), less commonly *aded* (' number '), may be inserted between number and noun without affecting the translation (like the Pidgin English ' piecee '): *iki bilet* or *iki tane bilet*, ' two tickets '. If the noun is not expressed, *tane* must be used: *Kaç bilet istiyorsunuz?—İki tane istiyorum*, ' How many tickets do you want?— I want two '. *baş* (' head ') is often used in the same way when enumerating livestock: *elli baş manda*, ' fifty (head) water-buffalo ';

otuz baş koyun, 'thirty sheep'. Note also *dört baş soğan.* 'four onions'.

(4) The rules of vowel harmony and consonant assimilation must be observed when writing figures: 'from five to seven', *beş-ten yedi-ye,* is written *5ten 7ye;* 'from nine to sixteen', *dokuz-dan on altı-ya,* is written *9dan 16ya.* 'In 1953' is *1953te.* In the example at the end of § 50, the *i* outside the bracket is the def. obj. case-ending of *on beş bin-i,* the number being the object of the verb *geçmiştir.*

(5) 'once, twice, three times', etc. Use *defa* or *kere,* 'time, occasion': *bir defa, iki defa, üç defa (bir kere,* etc.).

(6) In, e.g., 'one or two', 'or' is not translated: *Onu beş altı defa gördüm,* 'I've seen her five (or) six times'.

(7) *kırk,* 'forty', is used for an indefinitely high number, 'umpteen': *kırk yılda bir* ('in forty years one'), 'Once in a blue moon' Cf. § 160 (3).

Note (i): Besides 'hundred', *yüz* can mean 'face' or 'cause'. N.B. *iki-yüz-lü* (§ 86), 'two-faced'.

Note (ii): *Dörtler* ('the Fours') means 'the Four Great Powers'.

92. DEMONSTRATIVES

(1) *bu,* this (*next to the speaker*), this which precedes
şu, this, that (*just over there*), this which follows
o, that (*right over there* or *out of sight*)

o is also used for 'he, she, it', and the table of declension of *o* at § 70 serves as a model for *bu* and *şu* as well; they add the pronominal *n* before suffixes: *bundan,* 'from this', *şuna,* 'to that', *şunlar,* 'those'.

Like their English equivalents, these words are used as adjectives or pronouns:

o kitap, that book
o başka, that (is) different
bu saat-i buldunuz mu?, did you find this watch?
bunu buldunuz mu, did you find this?
şu askerler, those soldiers
şunlar asker değiller, those (people) aren't soldiers

(2) *böyle,* thus, in this way, like this, such
şöyle, thus, in this way, like this, such
öyle, thus, in that way, like that, such

The shades of meaning of these words are like those of *bu, şu* and *o*. They may be used adverbially:

> *böyle yaptım*, thus I did
> *öyle düşünüyor*, that's how he thinks

Or adjectivally:

> *böyle bir adam*, a man like this
> *şöyle bir gün*, such a day
> *öyle bir fırtına*, such a storm, a storm like that

93. POSTPOSITIONS

In English, words such as 'in', 'from', 'to', 'with' are called prepositions because they precede the noun to which they refer. As we have seen, 'of', 'to', 'from', 'at' are represented in Turkish by case-suffixes attached to the end of a word. Other English prepositions are represented by postpositions; suffixes or separate words *following* the word to which they refer.

Some postpositions require the word they govern to have a case-ending; compare the English use of the objective case with prepositions: 'to *whom*, by *me*, with *him*, like *her*' (not 'who, I, he, she').

94. POSTPOSITIONS WITH ABSOLUTE OR GENITIVE CASE

> *ile, -le/-la*, with, by means of   *gibi*, like
> *kadar*, as . . . as   *için*, for

(*a*) The pronouns *kim*, 'who?', *ben, sen, o, biz, siz, bu* and *şu* (§§ 70, 92), but not the plurals *onlar, bizler*, etc., take the genitive ending before these postpositions.   (*b*) Other words remain in the absolute form.

> (a) *kim-in ile* (*kiminle*), with whom?
>   *bu-nun gibi*, like this
>   *o-nun kadar güzel*, as beautiful as she
>   *siz-in için*, for you
> (b) *baba-nız ile* (*babanızla*), with your father
>   *bu adam gibi*, like this man
>   *o kız kadar güzel*, as beautiful as that girl
>   *sizler için*, for you

Note (*i*): *ile*. In conversation the unaccented suffixed form *-le/-la* is almost always used: *vapur-la*, 'by steamer'; *tren-le*, 'by train'. If attached to a word ending in a vowel, the form is *-yle/-yla* (cf. *idi*, § 82 (1)): *ustura-yla*, 'with the razor'; *kedi-yle*, with the cat '. It combines with the 3rd-person suffix -(s)i⁴ to form an invariable -iyle : kedi-siyle, ' with his cat '; babasiyle, ' with his father '; göziyle, ' with his eye '.

ile may be reinforced by berāber or birlikte, ' together ': Ahmet-le beraber geldim, ' I came, together with A. '; Kız-lar-la birlikte gittik, ' we went, along with the girls '.

bununla beraber (' together with this ') means ' in spite of this, nevertheless '.

Note (ii): gibi. gibi may take plural or possessive suffixes: bu gibiler ' (these likes), people of this sort '; o adam gibi-si-ni gördünüz mü? ' Have you seen the like of that man? '

Note (iii): kadar. This word is originally a noun meaning ' amount '. Used as a postposition without a following adjective it means ' as big as ', ' the size of ': bacak kadar bir çocuk (' leg-amount a child '), ' a child the size of a leg, knee-high '. After a number it means ' about ': on kadar uçak, ' about ten aircraft '. Bu kadar means ' this much '.

Note (iv): için. The suffixed form -çin is occasionally seen: senin-çin, ' for you '. A common use of için is to express purpose, with the infinitive: onu görmek için geldim, ' I came (for) to see him '. Compare ' I'm off to Louisiana for to see my Susie-Anna '.

Some uses of için overlap those of the dative case: bunu size (or sizin için) aldım, ' I bought this for you '. It also translates ' of ' in ' what do you think of him? ': onun için ne düşünüyorsunuz ?

95. TRANSLATION OF ' and '

The general equivalent is ve, but to join two nouns or pronouns together ile is more common: anne-m-le baba-m, ' my mother and my father '. ve is used: (a) before the last of a series of three or more words with the same grammatical function—annem, babam ve kardeşim, ' my mother, my father and my brother '; (b) between two adjectives: akıllı ve çalışkan bir talebe, ' an intelligent and industrious student '; (c) to join two main verbs—dükkân-a gitti ve kibrit aldı, ' he went to the shop and bought matches '.

de/da, properly ' also ', may often be rendered ' and '. This word must not be confused with the locative suffix; ' also ' is a separate word, and is never accented, while the locative suffix is written as part of the word it belongs to, and may be accented: siz de, ' you also, and you '; sizde, ' in you '.

A de B de means ' both A and B '.

Vocabulary 4

Days of the Week
pazar, Sunday
pazartesi, Monday
salı, Tuesday
çarşamba, Wednesday
perşembe, Thursday
cumā, Friday
cumartesi, Saturday

ad, isim (-smi), name
at (-tı), horse
ay, month, moon
bakan, minister
bilet (-ti), ticket
buz, ice
çarşı, market
çünkü, çünki, because
dünyā, world
erken, early
gece, night
gezmek, to stroll, go round, tour
(a place)

gün, day
güzel, beautiful, fine
hafta, week
hava, weather, air, climate
ıssız, lonely, deserted
karı, wife, woman
Kıbrıs, Cyprus
koca, husband
lâzım, necessary
mektup, letter
mesele, problem, question
ömür (-mrü), life
posta, post, mail
piyes, play (theatrical)
saç, hair
soğuk, cold
şey, thing
tayyāre, uçak, aeroplane
yağmur, rain
yarın, to-morrow
yoksa, or, otherwise
yol, road, way, journey

Exercise 4

(A) *Translate into English :* (1) Niçin bugün adalara gitmiyor-sunuz?—Çünkü hava güzel değil. (2) Bu mesele-yi sizin-le konuşmak istiyorduk. (3) Karı-m ile ben dün Kapalı Çarşı-yı gezdik. (4) Siz Türkiye'ye uçakla mı (tayyare ile mi) geldiniz yoksa vapurla mı? (5) Bu akşam için üç bilet-im var, bizim-le beraber geliyorsunuz değil mi?—Maalesef vaktim yok; yarın sabah Ankara'ya gidiyorum, bu gece erken yatmak istiyorum. (6) Yağmur-lu bir gece-de, iki at-lı ıssız bir yolda gidiyordu. (7) Ben ömrümde böyle bir şey görmedim. (8) Bir yılda (senede) on iki ay vardır. Bir ayda dört hafta vardır. Bir haftada yedi gün vardır. Günlerin isimleri (adları) şunlar-dır: pazar, pazartesi, salı, çarşamba, perşembe, cuma, cumartesi. Bunları öğrendiniz mi? (9) Dünyada İstanbul kadar güzel bir şehir var mı? (10) Bu mektub-u uçak posta-si-yle göndermek lâzım.

(B) *Translate into Turkish :* (1) My wife has gone to Cyprus in order to see her father. (2) Is that yellow-haired girl your sister? (3) My father and my brother did not like the new play. (4) How many tickets do you want to buy?—Five. (5) There are three hundred and sixty-five days in a year. (6) The new Minister is coming this morning by air (' by aeroplane ') from Istanbul. (7) This water is like ice; this water is as cold as ice. (8) Why are you strolling hatless and coatless in this weather? (9) Unfortunately my husband does not understand me. (10) Do you know that man? Why is he looking at us?

LESSON FIVE

96. Adverbs

(1) Turkish is not so fussy as English about the distinction between adjectives (which qualify nouns) and adverbs (which modify verbs). If your behaviour is *good*, you behave *well*; in Turkish, if your behaviour is *iyi*, you behave *iyi*.

(2) Words used adverbially may be repeated:

derin derin düşündüm, I thought deeply (deep deep)

yavaş yavaş gidiyorlar, they are going slowly (slow slow)

Note that in such doublets the accent is on the last syllable of the first element.

(3) There is also a suffix *-çe/-ça/-ce/-ca* (§ 44) which is used for making adverbs. This suffix is not accented:

güzel, beautiful; *güzelce*, beautifully, properly

lisan, dil, language; *lisanca, dilce*, linguistically

hükûmet, government; *hükûmetçe*, governmentally, on the part of the government

ben, I; *bence*, for my part, to my mind

doğru, straight; *doğruca*, directly

Words which show the pronominal *n* before case-endings show it also before this suffix: *bu*, ' this '; *bunca*, ' in this way, this much '.

Türkçe konuşmak, which we translate ' to speak Turkish ', really means ' to speak in-the-Turkish-way '. Words so formed, by adding *-ce* to nouns of nationality, though strictly adverbs, are used as adjectives—*İngilizce sözlük*, ' English dictionary '—or nouns—*Fransızca-m zayıf*, ' my French is weak '.

97. Adverbs of Place

These are formed by adding to the demonstratives (§ 92) or to *ne* ' what? ' the syllable *re/ra*, followed by the appropriate case-ending. The accent is on the first syllable of the word so formed:

bu-ra-da, in this place, here; *ne-re-de* (*nerde*), in what place, where?

bu-ra-dan, from this place, hence; *ne-re-den* (*nerden*), from what place, whence?

bu-ra-ya, to this place, hither; *ne-re-ye*, to what place, whither?

So too: *orada, oradan, oraya; şurada, şuradan, şuraya*, there, thence, thither.

But as ' hither, hence, whence ', etc., are not in use in spoken English, care must be taken to add the right suffix when translating into Turkish:

> Where are you? *Nerede-siniz?*
> Where are you going? *Nereye gidiyorsunuz?*
> Where have you come from? *Nereden geldiniz?*
> He is standing there, *Şurada duruyor.*
> He is going there, *Şuraya gidiyor.*
> He has left (gone from) there, *Şuradan gitti.*

Bu-ra, etc., are not used nowadays in the absolute form. If we want to say, e.g., ' This place is beautiful ', it is usual to add the 3rd-person suffix: *Burası güzel* (' this-its-place '). *Burası neresi?* ' What place is this? '. Radio Ankara identifies itself thus: *Burası Ankara Türkiye*, ' This (place) is Ankara, Turkey '.

Note (i): The heading of this paragraph refers to the *English* grammatical category. *orada, buraya*, etc., are no more adverbs than are *odada*, ' in the room ', or *sinemaya*, ' to the pictures '.

Note (ii): *-li* (§ 86) may be used with *-re/-ra*: *Nereli-siniz?* (' you are characterized-by-what-place? '), ' where are you from?' *Ben İstanbul-lu-yum. Siz de oralı mısınız?* ' I'm an Istanbul man. Are you a-native-of-that-place too?'

Note (iii): The words described above may take the plural suffix: *burada*, ' here '; *buralarda*, ' in these parts '; *oralarda*, ' thereabouts '. Note also *uzak-ta* and *uzaklarda*, ' far off '; *yakın-da* and *yakınlarda*, ' near by, soon, recently '.

98. THE SUFFIX *-ki*

-ki (see § 37 (2)) may be added:

(1) To the genitive case of a noun or pronoun, to make a pronoun meaning ' the one which is . . .' whatever precedes:

> *benim*, of me; *benimki*, the one which is of me, mine
> *Ahmed-in-ki*, the one which belongs to Ahmet
> *onlar-ın-ki*, theirs

(2) To the locative case of a noun or pronoun, or to an adverb of place or time. The resulting word may be used as pronoun or adjective:

> *bugün*, to-day; *bugünkü gazete*, to-day's newspaper
> *burada*, here; *buradaki kitap*, the book which is here; *buradakiler*, those who are here
> *oda-m-da*, in my room; *odamdaki telefon*, the telephone which is in my room; *sizin odanızdaki*, the one in your room

Any case-endings added to pronouns formed with *-ki* are preceded by the pronominal *n*:

> *benimkinden*, from mine
> *onunkinin*, of his
> *sizinkine*, to yours
> *bizimkinde*, in ours
> *onlarınkini aldı*, he took theirs

99. COMPARISON OF ADJECTIVES AND ADVERBS

(1) *daha*, more; *en*, most.

uzun, long	*iyi*, good, well	*çok*, much
daha uzun, longer	*daha iyi*, better	*daha çok*, more
en uzun, longest	*en iyi*, best	*en çok*, most

> *az*, little; *az faydalı* (little useful), of little use
> *daha az*, less; *daha az faydalı*, less useful
> *en az*, least; *en az faydalı*, least useful

'than' is expressed by the ablative suffix; for 'this is better than that' Turkish says 'this is better *from* that'—Example (*a*). In sentences containing a 'than', *daha* may be omitted—Example (*b*). It cannot be omitted if there is no 'than'—Example (*c*).

Examples:

(a) *Bu, şundan daha iyi-dir*⎫
(b) *Bu, şundan iyidir*   ⎬ This is better than that.

(c) *Şunu beğenmiyorum ; bu daha iyidir*, I don't like that; this is better.

Evimiz sizin-ki-n-den (daha) az rutubetlidir, Our house is less damp than yours.

Dünya-nın en yüksek tepe-si Himalâyalardadır. The world's highest peak is in the Himalayas.

(2) Apart from the use of *en*, Turkish has two methods of making superlatives: (*a*) by repetition (cf. § 96 (2)):

> *derin düşünceler*, deep thoughts; *derin derin düşünceler*, profound thoughts
>
> *garip hareketler*, strange actions; *garip garip hareketler*, extraordinary actions

(*b*) by prefixing a syllable resembling the first syllable of the word but ending in *m, p, s* or *r*. This prefix is accented:

> *başka*, other; *bambaşka*, totally different
> *temiz*, clean; *tertemiz*, spotless
> *siyah*, black; *simsiyah*, jet black
> *bütün*, whole; *büsbütün*, entirely
> *doğru*, straight; *dosdoğru*, dead straight
> *yeni*, new; *yepyeni*, brand new
> *kırmızı*, red; *kıpkırmızı*, bright red

100. USES OF THE ABLATIVE CASE

(1) The ablative indicates the point of origin or departure. Hence its use in comparisons: *bu şundan büyüktür*, ' this is bigger than that ', might be rendered ' this, taking that as starting-point, is big '. Hence also its use with verbs denoting avoidance, separation, withdrawal (' from '). It indicates the cause from which something proceeds: *bu sebepten*, ' for this reason '; *ondan korkuyorum*, ' I am afraid of him ' (my fearing arises *from* him). *Gitmedim*; *para-m yok-tu da on-dan*, ' I didn't go; I had no money, that's why ' (' and from that '). It translates ' of ' as in ' one of the children ': *çocuklar-dan bir-i* (' from the children, one-of-them '); and in ' I have no news of him ': *on-dan haber-im yok*. ' I am sure of this ': *bundan emin-im*. It indicates the material *out of* which something is made: *yeni masa-yı ceviz-den yapıyor*, ' he is making the new table *of* walnut '.

(2) English ' through, by way of ' is rendered by the ablative: *buradan geçmediler*, ' they did not pass through here '; *pencere-den bakıyor*, ' she is looking through the window '; *köprüye bu yol-dan gitti*, ' he went to the bridge by this road '; *elim-den tuttu*, ' he held me *by* my hand ' (*elim-i tuttu* would be ' he held my hand ').

(3) Some adverbs are formed with the ablative suffix, e.g., *sonradan*, ' afterwards '; *önceden*, ' beforehand '; *eskiden*, ' in the old days ' (*not* ' from . . . '); *çoktan*, ' long since '; *sahiden*, ' really, truly '. N.B. *doğru-dan doğru-ya*, ' directly '.

Note : Words construed with the ablative will be shown preceded by *-den*, of course as an abbreviation for ' *-den* or *-dan* according to vowel harmony '. As a reminder that the ablative is required with certain words, the beginner may find it helpful to memorize, for example, *-den korkmak*, ' to fear ', as ' to be afraid from '.

Similarly, words construed with the dative will be shown preceded by *-e*.

101. Postpositions with Ablative Case

> *-den evvel*, *-den önce*, before
> *-den sonra*, after
> *-den dolayı*, *-den ötürü*, on account of, because of
> *-den beri* (see *Notes*), since, for the last . . .
> *-den başka*, other than, apart from, besides

Distinguish between *-den evvel*, *önce*, *sonra* and the same words used with the absolute case :

> *üç gün evvel* (*önce*), three days before, ago
> *bundan evvel* (*önce*), before this
> *iki saat sonra*, two hours after, later
> *salı-dan sonra*, after Tuesday
> *o günden dört gün sonra*, four days after that day

Note (*i*) : The present tense is used of activity that began in the past and is still going on, just as in French (which is why one may hear Continental visitors saying, ' I am in London since three weeks '). *Ocak-tan beri Ankara'da oturuyorum*, ' I have been living in A. since January. *İki ay-dan beri Banka-da çalışıyor*, ' For the last two months (since two months) he has been working at the Bank.'

Note (*ii*) : *beri* is sometimes written as a suffix : *iki aydanberi*.

102. The Verb : Future and Future-past Tenses

The tense-suffix is *-ecek/-acak*, to which are added the ' I am/ was ' endings (cf. § 88). Remember that *k* before a vowel becomes *ğ*. Here are the future and future-past tenses of *gitmek* (*gid-*), ' to go ' :

gideceğim, I shall go	*gidecektim*, I was about to go *or* I should go (if . . .)
gideceksin, thou wilt go	*gidecektin*, thou wert about to go, etc.
gidecek(tir), he will go	*gidecekti*, he was about to go

gideceğiz, we shall go

gideceksiniz, you will go

gidecekler, they will go

gidecektik, we were about to go

gidecektiniz, you were about to go

gidecektiler } they were about to go
gideceklerdi }

The Negative and Interrogative are formed as shown in §§ 89, 90 :

gitmiyeceğim, I shall not go

gitmiyecek misiniz? will you not go?

gidecek miydik? were we about to go?

gitmiyecek miydiniz? weren't you about to go?

gitmiyecekler mi? will they not go?

Note : We do not usually say ' You will come and you will see . . .', but ' You will come and see . . .' So in Turkish there is no need to say *geleceksiniz ve göreceksiniz*; it is enough to say *gelecek, göreceksiniz* (' about-to-come, about-to-see you are '). This may be done with any tense except the past tense in *-di* (§ 81): cf. § 123.

103. COMPOUND VERBS

There are a large number of expressions in common use made up of a noun (often non-Turkish in origin) and the verb *etmek* (*ed-*), ' to do ':

kabul etmek (to do acceptance), to accept

teşkil etmek (to do forming), to constitute

telefon etmek (to do telephone), to telephone

In the older language, other words for ' to do ' were used in such compounds, notably *eylemek* and *kılmak*. The former is still in written use, especially to avoid the constant repetition of *etmek* (e.g., Exercise 14, sentence 18). The only compound in which *kılmak* is used nowadays is *namaz kılmak*, ' to perform the rites of (Muslim) prayer '.

The main accent in such compounds is on the last syllable of the noun, except when the interrogative *mi* follows, when the last syllable before the *mi* has the main accent: *telefon ediyor*, ' he is 'phoning ', but *telefon ediyor mu?* ' is he 'phoning? '

If the noun of such a compound is liable to a sound change before a vowel (§§ 43, 45, 47), it is usually written as one word with the *etmek* or *eylemek* :

ayırt, distinction; *ayırdetmek*, to distinguish

af (*-ffı*), pardon; *affetmek*, to pardon

sabır (*-brı*), patience, endurance; *sabretmek*, to be patient

(*ayırdeylemek, affeylemek, sabreylemek*)

104. ' It's raining '

Turkish always supplies a subject for *yağmak*, ' to rain ', and *gürlemek*, ' to thunder ' :

> *yağmur yağıyor* (rain is raining), it's raining
> *dolu yağıyor* (hail is raining), it's hailing
> *kar yağıyor* (snow is raining), it's snowing
> *gök gürlüyor* (sky is thundering), it's thundering

Vocabulary 5

acaba, I wonder
bahis (-hsi), discussion, topic;
  -den bahsetmek, to speak of, mention
çiçek, flower
durum, vaziyet, position, situation
geniş, wide, spacious
gül, rose (flower)
hal (§ 64), condition, state
hem A hem B (or *hem de B*), both A and B
her, every; *herhalde*, in any case, certainly
iktisādī, economic
kadın, woman, lady
kara,* siyah, black
kim? who?
koku, smell, scent

köpek, dog
köşe, corner
lokanta, restaurant
meclis, assembly
millet (-ti), nation, religious community
muvaffak, successful
nihayet, at last
resim (-smi), picture
tātil, holiday
teklif, proposal, motion
tiyatro, theatre
toplantı, meeting
yardım, help; *-e yardım etmek*, to help
yaz, summer
yorulmak, to be tired, to weary oneself

Exercise 5

(A) *Translate into English :* (1) Çalışacak, yorulacak ve nihayet muvaffak olacaksınız. (2) Oradaki kara otomobil kim-in?—Bilmiyorum herhalde benimki değil. (3) Arkadaşınız nereli-dir?—O, benim gibi, Londra-lı-dır. (4) Yakında mı Türkiye'ye gideceksiniz?—Pek yakında değil, yaz tatil-i-nden sonra gideceğim. (5) Babanız bugünkü trenle mi gidiyor, yoksa yarın-a mı kalıyor? (6) İstanbul hem en büyük, hem de en güzel şehr-imiz-dir. (7) Şu resim, benim oda-m-da-ki gibidir, değil mi?—Evet, fakat

* Besides *kara*, ' black ', there is a noun *kara* meaning ' land ': *kara kuvvetleri*, ' land-forces '; *kara suları*, ' territorial waters '; *kara-ya çıkmak*, ' to disembark ' (' go-out to-the-land ').

sizin-ki-n-den daha güzel-dir. (8) Niçin oturdunuz da bana
yardım etmediniz? (9) Şu iki kadından siyah-lı-sı Başbakan-ın
karı-sı-dır. (10) Büyük Millet Meclis-i (B.M.M.) bu teklif-i
kabul edecek mi acaba?—Etmiyecek. (11) Bu mesele-den
bahsetmiyecek miydiniz? (12) Ben bu sabah kardeşim-den
evvel kalktım

(B) *Translate into Turkish :* (1) We weren't going to go to the
theatre, on account of to-morrow's meeting. (2) What is that
man in the corner doing, I wonder?—He's praying, isn't he?
(3) Did the Grand National Assembly not accept the Minister's
motion? (4) Our economic situation is now totally different.
(5) After the theatre, we went to the Station Restaurant. (6)
Orhan is both the biggest and the most intelligent of the children.
—Is he more intelligent than his own sister, I wonder? (7) Were
you speaking of to-day's meeting? (8) His room is not as clean
as mine; mine's spotless. (9) I held the child by the hand, and
we passed together across Galata Bridge. (10) What's the name
of your brother's dog?—He has no dog; the name of mine is
Karabash. (11) In my opinion, the flower with the most beautiful
scent is the rose. (12) At last we've found a house with a spacious
garden.

LESSON SIX

105. THE VERB—AORIST TENSES

The aorist ('unbounded') tenses, present and past, express habitual or continuous activity: 'he goes to school', 'she used to live in France'. The tense-suffix is *-r*, added directly to vowel stems:

> *anla-mak*, to understand; *anlar*, he understands
> *taşı-mak*, to carry; *taşır*, he carries

A vowel is inserted between the *r* and consonant-stems, according to the following rules:

(1) Consonant-stems of one syllable form their aorist by adding *-er/-ar*:

> *et-mek*, to do; *ed-er*, he does
> *git-mek* to go; *gid-er*, he goes
> *çık-mak*, to go up, out; *çık-ar*, he goes up, out
> *sor-mak*, to ask; *sor-ar*, he asks

Exceptions (all these are common and must be known):

> Aorist in *-ır*: *almak*, to take; *kalmak*, to remain; *sanmak*, to think; *varmak*, to reach: *alır, kalır, sanır, varır*.
> Aorist in *-ur*: *olmak*, to be, become; *bulmak*, to find; *durmak*, to stand; *vurmak*, to strike: *olur, bulur, durur, vurur*.
> Aorist in *-ir*: *gelmek*, to come; *vermek*, to give; *bilmek*, to know: *gelir, verir, bilir*.
> Aorist in *-ür*: *görmek*, to see; *ölmek*, to die: *görür, ölür*.

(2) Consonant-stems of more than one syllable add *-ir*[4]:

> *kullan-mak*, to use; *kullan-ır*, he uses
> *çalış-mak*, to work, try; *çalış-ır*, he works, tries
> *göster-mek*, to show; *göster-ir*, he shows
> *getir-mek*, to bring; *getir-ir*, he brings
> *dokun-mak*, to touch; *dokun-ur*, he touches
> *öksür-mek*, to cough; *öksür-ür*, he coughs

64

(3) To these aorist bases are added the ' I am/was ' endings, with the exception of *dir* (cf. § 88):

gösteririm, I show	*gösterirdim*, I used to show, should show (if . . .)
gösterirsin, thou showest	*gösterirdin*, thou didst show
gösterir, he shows	*gösterirdi*, he used to show
gösteririz, we show	*gösterirdik*, we used to show
gösterirsiniz, you show	*gösterirdiniz*, you used to show
gösterirler, they show	*gösterirlerdi* *gösterirdiler* } they used to show

So also: *görürüm, görürsün*, etc., ' I see '; *bulurum, bulursun*, etc., ' I find '; *kullanırdım*, ' I used to use '; *öksürürdünüz*, ' you used to cough '.

106. THE AORIST NEGATIVE

Unlike other tenses, the negative of the aorist is formed by adding to the negative stem (§ 83) not the tense-suffix *r* but a *z*, which is omitted in the 1st person singular and plural. A further irregularity is in the accentuation. The following models should therefore be learned by heart:

gelmemek, not to come	*almamak*, not to take
gelmem, I do not come	*almam*, I do not take
gelmezsin, thou dost not come	*almazsın*, thou dost not take
gelmez, he does not come	*almaz*, he does not take
gelmeyiz, we do not come	*almayız*, we do not take
gelmezsiniz, you do not come	*almazsınız*, you do not take
gelmezler, they do not come	*almazlar*, they do not take

The aorist past is formed by adding *-dim*, *-din*, etc., to the negative aorist base: *gelmezdim, gelmezdin, gelmezdi, gelmezdik, gelmezdiniz, gelmezlerdi* or *gelmezdiler*, ' I used not to come ', etc.

The interrogative is regular—*miyim, mivdim*, etc., following the base, positive or negative:

> *gelir misiniz?* do you come?
> *gelmez miydiniz?* used you not to come?
> *almaz mıydık?* used we not to take?

C

107. Uses of the Aorist

(1) Statements of general validity:

kahve severim, I like coffee
iki iki daha dört eder, two plus two make four (two, two more, make four)

(2) Expressions of willingness or readiness (compare 'We go anywhere, do anything'):

Bana bir kibrit ver-ir misiniz? Will you give me a match?
Evet, ver-ir-im, Yes I will.

It is therefore used to express promises: *Gelirim dedim mi, gelirim ben*, ' " I'll come " did I say? (Then) I'll come '.

(3) Sometimes the present and aorist tenses seem to be used indifferently; *biliyorum* or *bilirim*, ' I know '. Practice is the best guide, but here is a working rule:

oku-yor-um, I am reading
oku-r-um, I read *or* I shall read
oku-yacağ-ım, I am going to read

oku-yor-dum, I was reading
oku-r-dum, I used to read
oku-yacak-tım, I was going to read

Note (i): *affedersiniz* ('you pardon'), 'I beg your pardon'; *teşekkür ederim* ('I do thank'), 'thank you'; *olur* ('it comes to be'), 'it is possible, all right, O.K.'; *olmaz* ('it does not come to be'), 'it is impossible, it won't do'.

Note (ii): *istemez*, ' he does not want ', is colloquially used for ' I don't want it ', e.g., when shaking off importunate street-traders. It is conventionally explained as being short for *can istemez*, ' (My) soul does not want '.

108. 'While'

'While' is translated by the invariable and unaccented suffix *-ken* or the separate word *iken*, strictly ' while being ', the *i-* being the stem of the old verb ' to be ' (§ 82), both commonly used after the aorist base, as in the first two examples:

Üsküdar'a gider iken (giderken) bir mendil buldum, While going to Scutari, I found a handkerchief.
O hiç şarap içmezken dün akşam bir şişe içti, While he never drinks wine, yesterday evening he drank a bottle.
Askerken Kıbrıs'a gittim, While I was in the Army (soldier-while) I went to Cyprus.

Vaktiniz var iken, niçin bu makale-yi okumazsınız? While you
have the time (your-time existent while-being), why
don't you read this article?

Note that the subject of the 'while' clause is not shown by
the aorist, which remains in the base-form, but has to be indicated
externally; in the first example it is 'I', the subject of the main
verb *buldum*, in the second it is 'he': *O*.

109. 'As soon as'

The positive and negative aorist bases used together mean 'as
soon as':

> *Ben gelir gelmez, Ahmet çıktı,* As soon as I came, Ahmet went
> out (I coming not-coming, i.e., when I was on the
> dividing line between arrival and non-arrival).
>
> *Mektub-unuz-u alır almaz baba-m-a gösterdim,* As soon as I
> received your letter I showed (it) to my father.

Note : But *ister istemez* means 'willy-nilly', while *olur olmaz*
means 'any old . . ., just any . . .': *Bu iş ister istemez olacak,*
'This thing is going to be, like it or not'. *Bu, olur olmaz adam-ın
kâr-ı değil,* 'This isn't just any man's job'.

110. NUMERALS: ORDINAL

(1) In § 91 we saw the Turkish equivalents of 'one, two, three',
etc., the cardinal numerals. Ordinal numerals—'first, second,
third'—are formed by adding -*nci*[4] to cardinal numerals ending
in a vowel, -*inci*[4] to those ending in a consonant:

birinci, first	*sekizinci*, eighth
ikinci, second	*dokuzuncu*, ninth
üçüncü, third	*onuncu*, tenth
dördüncü, fourth	*yirminci*, twentieth
beşinci, fifth	*bininci*, thousandth
altıncı, sixth	*otuz beşinci*, thirty-fifth
yedinci, seventh	

(2) Besides *birinci*, *ilk* also is used for 'first', 'primary'.
'Last' is *son*, which as a noun means 'end'.

(3) From *kaç*, 'how many?' is formed *kaçıncı*, 'how-manyeth?':

> *Oğlunuz sınıf-ı-nın kaçıncı-sı-dır?* (Your-son of-his-class is-its-
> how-manyeth), What's your son's position in class?

(4) Just as we abbreviate ' first, second, third ', etc., to 1st, 2nd, 3rd and so on, the Turkish equivalents are abbreviated to *1inci*, *2inci*, *3üncü*, sometimes to *1ci*, *2ci*, *3cü*, etc. With names of sovereigns, the Roman numerals are used: *Mehmet II*, pronounced *ikinci Mehmet*. Some writers have the logical, but at first sight confusing, habit of putting the numeral first: *II Mehmet*, *VI Corç* (§ 42), *II Elizabet*.

111. FRACTIONS

There are three words for ' half ':

(1) *buçuk* is used only with whole numbers, and must always be translated ' and a half ': *iki buçuk*, ' 2½ '; *kırk dokuz buçuk*, ' 49½ '.

(2) *yarı* is used—

    (*a*) as a noun—*şu kitapların yar.-sı türkçe*, ' half of those books are Turkish '; *gece yarısı* (' night its-half '), ' midnight '.

    (*b*) as an adjective, to be translated ' mid- '—*yarı gece*, ' midnight '.

    (*c*) as an adverb, modifying adjectives—*yarı deli*, ' half-mad '; *yarı yuvarlak*, ' half-round '.

(3) *yarım* is an adjective meaning ' half ':

    bir yarım saat, a half-hour
    bir yarım elma, a half-apple
    yarımada, peninsula (half-island)

' Quarter ' is *çeyrek*, little used except with *saat*: *bir çeyrek saat*, ' a quarter-hour, a quarter of an hour '.

Other fractions are put in the form ' one in five ', ' three in seven ': *beş-te bir*, ' ⅕ '; *yedi-de üç*, ' 3/7 '; *yüzde on*, ' 10/100 '.

    para-nın dörtte bir-i (of the money, in four its-one), a quarter of the money

    köylü-ler-in yüz-de doksan-ı, ninety per cent of the villagers

As the *yüzde*, ' in hundred, per cent ', comes first, so too does the percentage sign: % 90.

112. ' Two each '

Distributive numerals are formed by adding *-er/-ar* to numbers ending in a consonant, *-şer/-şar* to those ending in a vowel: *birer*, *ikişer*, *üçer*, *dörder*, *beşer*, *altışar*, ' one each, two each, three each ', etc. ' Half each ' is irregular: *yarımşar*. *Çocuklara bir elma* *verdim*, ' I gave the children an apple ', but *çocuklara birer elma verdim*, ' I gave the children an apple each '.

> *Bize kırk beşer lira verdi*, He gave us £45 each.
> *Askerler üçer üçer yürüyorlar* (cf. § 96 (2)), The soldiers are marching in threes, three by three.

113. THE SUFFIX *-ci*

-ci/-çi[4] denotes regular occupation or profession, like our ' -ist '.

> *telgraf*, telegraph; *telgrafçı*, telegraphist
> *kapı*, door, gate; *kapıcı*, porter, doorkeeper
> *süt*, milk; *sütçü*, milkman
> *tütün*, tobacco; *tütüncü*, tobacconist
> *spor*, sports, games; *sporcu*, sportsman, athlete
> *yalan*, falsehood; *yalancı*, liar, imitation
> *inat*, obstinacy; *inatçı*, pig-headed
> *yol*, road, way; *yolcu*, traveller
> *eski*, old; *eskici*, rag-and-bone man
> *milliyet*, nationality; *milliyetçi*, nationalist
> *ne?* what?; *neci?* of what profession?

114. THE SUFFIX *-lik*

(1) Its most important use is to make abstract nouns:

> *güzel*, beautiful; *güzellik*, beauty
> *çocuk*, child; *çocukluk*, childhood, childishness
> *akılsız*, unintelligent; *akılsızlık*, stupidity
> *sıcak*, hot; *sıcaklık*, heat
> *asker*, soldier; *askerlik*, military service
> *ben*, I; *benlik*, identity, personality
> *bir*, one; *birlik*, unity, unit, union
> *milliyetçi*, nationalist; *milliyetçilik*, nationalism
> *yolcu*, traveller; *yolculuk*, travel, travelling

(2) Another common use is to make adjectives and nouns from numerical expressions:

> *kişi*, person; *yemek*, food; *üç kişilik yemek*, food for three people
> *posta pul-u*, postage-stamp; *beş kuruşluk posta pul-ları*, five-piastre stamps
> *gün*, day; *iki günlük yol*, two-day journey
> *ihtiyar*, old (man); *seksenlik bir ihtiyar*, an old man of eighty

(3) It makes adjectives and nouns showing the purpose for which something is intended or suitable:

kömür, coal; *kömürlük,* coal-hole, bunker

odun, wood; *odunluk,* wood-shed, -pile

saman, straw; *samanlık,* straw-rick

kumaş, material; *perde,* curtain; *perdelik kumaş,* curtaining material

gelin, bride; *gelinlik kızlar,* marriageable girls

cennet, paradise; *cennetlik,* destined for paradise

cehennem, hell; *cehennemlik,* (*a*) destined for hell, (*b*) stokehold of a Turkish bath

korku, fear; *korkuluk,* scarecrow

göz, eye; *gözlük,* eyeglasses, spectacles

evlât, child; *evlâtlık,* adopted child

Note (*i*): *şimdilik, bugünlük* ('for now, for to-day') are used adverbially: *Şimdilik Allaha ısmarladık* (§ 177), 'Good-bye for now'. *Bugünlük bu kadar yeter,* 'That's enough for to-day (this amount suffices for to-day').

Note (*ii*): The word 'odalisque' is from the Turkish *odalık,* '(girl) for the (bed-) room'.

115. Uses of the Dative Case

The dative shows the recipient or destination, the point *to* which an action is directed. It is therefore common with verbs of motion and with adjectives conveying such ideas as proximity and conformity. Usually it may be translated 'to', but sometimes English idiom demands a different preposition, as shown by the italicized words in the English of the following examples. Examples 8 to 12 show some Turkish verbs which take a dative, although their English equivalents have a direct object.

1. *Bu çiçekleri siz-e aldım,* I bought these flowers *for* you.
2. *Resimler-e bakıyor,* She is looking *at* the pictures.
3. *Hastalar-a bakar,* She looks *after* the patients.
4. *Kalemi cebim-e koydum,* I put the pen *into* my pocket.
5. *Et-e tuz koydum,* I put salt *on* the meat.
6. *Sandālye-ye (yerim-e) oturdum,* I sat down *on* the chair (*in* my place).
7. *Pusula-ya adresini yazdı,* He wrote his address *on* the chit.
8. *Kardeşiniz siz-e benziyor,* Your brother resembles you.
9. *Oda-ya girdik,* We entered the room.

10. *İşimiz-e başladık*, We began our work.
11. *Vapur-a bindim*, I boarded the steamer.
12. *Köy-e vardık*, We reached the village.

For the dative expressing purpose, see §§ 125 (*neye?*) and 130 (*a*).
The infinitive may be governed by a verb taking the dative:

yürümeğ-e başladık, we began to walk.

116. POSTPOSITIONS WITH THE DATIVE CASE

The meaning of the dative may be made more specific by means
of a postposition:

-e göre, according to, suitable for, applicable to, fitting
-e kadar (the amount to), as far as, until (see *Notes*)
-e doğru (straight to), towards
-e karşı (opposite to), against, facing
-e rağmen, in spite of

Note (*i*): *-e kadar* also translates ' in ', as in ' he will come *in*
five minutes ', *beş dakika-ya kadar gelecek*, and ' by ' as in ' If you
are not back *by* ten we'll go without you '. For an example see
Exercise 12, (A) (3).

Note (*ii*): Instead of *-e kadar*, some writers use the archaic and
provincial *-e dek*: *sabah-a dek konuştuk*, ' we talked until morning '.

117. VERBS, TRANSITIVE AND INTRANSITIVE

A verb is said to be used transitively when its action passes over
(' transits ') to a direct object—' I ate a bun '—and intransitively
when there is no object expressed—' When did you last eat? '
Some verbs are never transitive: ' he exists, we intervened '. In
Turkish, when a normally transitive verb is used without a direct
object there is a tendency to supply a cognate object in the shape
of a noun from the same root as the verb. Here are some common examples: *yazı yazmak* (' to write writing '), ' to write ';
yemek yemek, ' to eat ' (the first *yemek* is a noun meaning ' eating,
meal, food ', the second is the infinitive ' to eat '): *dikiş dikmek*, ' to
sew '; *örgü örmek*, ' to knit '. In the (*a*) sentences following, the
verb has an external direct object; in the (*b*) sentences there is
no external object, so a cognate object is supplied.

1. (a) *Babam, odasında mektuplarını yazıyor*, My father is
   writing his letters in his room.
   (b) *Babam, odasında yazı yazıyor*, My father is writing in
   his room.

2. (a) *Bugün et yemedim,* I have not eaten meat to-day.
   (b) *Bugün yemek yemedim,* I have not eaten to-day.
3. (a) *Karım gömleğimi dikiyor,* My wife is sewing my shirt.
   (b) *Karım dikiş dikiyor,* My wife is sewing.
4. (a) *Annem bana bir kazak örüyor,* My mother is knitting a
      pullover for me.
   (b) *Annem örgü örüyor,* My mother is knitting.

118. MONTHS OF THE YEAR

ocak, January	*temmuz,* July
şubat, February	*ağustos,* August
mart (-tı), March	*eylûl,* September
nisan, April	*ekim,* October
mayıs, May	*kasım,* November
haziran, June	*aralık,* December

For four of the months, older names are still met with:

ikinci kânun, son kânun or *kânûnusâni,* January
birinci teşrin, ilk teşrin or *teşrinievvel,* October
ikinci teşrin, son teşrin or *teşrinisâni,* November
birinci kânun, ilk kânun or *kânûnuevvel,* December

' In May ' is *mayıs-ta* or *mayıs ay-ı-nda.* ' On the first of the
month ' is *ay-ın bir-i-nde* (' on the one of the month '). ' On the
eighth of March ' is *sekiz mart-ta,* written *8 martta.* Roman
figures are often used to indicate the month, and the thousands
figure of the year is often omitted: *20. vi. 953,* ' 20th June 1953 '.

Vocabulary 6

apart(ı)man, flat, block of flats
ayak, foot; *ayakkabı,* footwear,
  pair of shoes (§ 75 (4))
banka, bank
basmak, to press, print; *-e
  basmak,* to tread on
-e binmek, to mount, board
biraz, a little
cihan, world
değişmek, to change (intransitive)
dolap, cupboard
dolaşmak, to walk about, roam,
  go round

ekmek, bread
fâiz, interest (bank)
fotoğraf, photograph
gâlibâ, presumably, I believe
gene, yine, again, moreover
harp (-rbi), war
hasta, ill
hayhay, certainly!
hesap, account (bank)
insan, human being, man
kalem, pen
kâğıt, paper
kazanmak, to win, gain

kişi, person (usually with a number)
-den korkmak, to be afraid of
kuruş, piastre
kuş, bird
küçük, small
lútfen (first word in sentence), please!
manav, fruiterer
meydan, open space, square
muhārebe, battle, war; meydan muhārebesi, pitched battle
mürekkep, ink
nesil (-sli), generation
ordu, army

öğle, noon
paha, price; pahalı, expensive
portakal, orange
radyo, radio, wireless
raf, shelf
rahat, comfortable
şüphe, doubt
takım, team, set, gang
tam, exactly, just
tasarruf, savings
tramvay, tram
uğramak, to drop in, call
vagon, railway-carriage
zaman, time; ne zaman, when?

Exercise 6

(A) *Translate into English :* (1) On bir-er kişilik iki takım. (2) Siz bir yarım saat beklediniz, biz bir buçuk saat bekledik. (3) Ekmeğ-in yarı-sı-nı kim yedi? (4) Bu portakal-lar-ı dörder kuruş-a aldım. Manav biraz daha büyüklerine yedişer kuruş istedi, pahalı buldum da almadım. (5) Bankalar küçük tasarruf hesaplarına yüzde iki buçuk faiz verirler. (6) Sene-nin ilk kar-ı dün yağdı. (7) Son cihan harbi ne zaman başladı?—Üç eylûl 1939da. (8) Ben gene belki yarın öğleden sonra uğra-r-ım. (9) Türk ordusu 30 ağustos 1922de dünyanın en büyük meydan muharebelerinden birini kazandı. (10) Yatak-lı vagonda yolculuk şüphe-siz çok rahat bir şey. (11) Üçüncü raf-ta-ki kâğıtlar kim-in? (12) Galiba ayağınız-a bastım. Affedersiniz, görmedim.

(B) *Translate into Turkish :* (1) Will you please bring me the telephone-directory?—Certainly!—Thank you. (2) In order to write, pen, paper and ink are necessary. (3) I walked about till evening; I did not find a pair of shoes to fit my foot. (4) Aren't you afraid of becoming ill? (5) As soon as we saw the tram, Orhan began to run. (6) Your clock is standing on the second shelf of that cupboard. (7) While I was boarding the tram this morning in Taksim Square I saw three photographers. (8) This flat is just suitable for you. (9) My wife sews while listening to the wireless. (10) Man, by means of the aeroplane, flies in the air like the birds (§ 53). (11) Every great city changes from generation to generation. (12) She's gone; I don't know where.

LESSON SEVEN

119. PARTICIPLES AND VERBAL NOUNS

A participle is an adjective formed from a verb (it *partakes* of the nature of both adjective and verb). English has a present and a past participle; present, as in ' the glory is *departing* ' and past, as in ' the glory is *departed* '. It is unfortunate for our purposes that in English present participles and verbal nouns have the same suffix ' -ing '; in Turkish they have different suffixes, so the distinction must be clearly understood.

> (*a*) His brother is swimming.
> (*b*) His recreation is swimming.

In (*a*), ' swimming ' is a participle, a verbal adjective for which we may substitute other adjectives: ' his brother is fat, energetic, clever, married '. In (*b*), ' swimming ' is a verbal noun, for which we may substitute other nouns: ' his recreation is tennis, music, woodwork '.

The -*mek*/-*mak* infinitive is one form of verbal noun; we may translate *düşmek kolaydır* as ' to fall is easy ' or ' falling is easy '.

120. ' The man *who is walking* in the street.'
   ' The letter *which will come* to-morrow.'
   ' The woman *who has bought* this shop.'

Such expressions are rendered in Turkish by means of participles, thus: ' In-the-street *walking* man ' (§ 65 (4)), ' To-morrow *being-about-to-come* letter ', ' This shop *having-bought* woman '.

121. PRESENT PARTICIPLE

-(*y*)*en*/-(*y*)*an* suffixed to verb-stem: *olmak*, ' to be '; *olan*, ' being, who or which is '; *olmamak*, ' not to be ', *olmyan*, ' not being, who or which is not '; *yürümek*, ' to walk ', *yürüyen*, ' walking ', etc., *yürümüyen*, ' not walking ', etc.

The present participle represents action contemporaneous with the main verb, so it is sometimes to be translated as past:

> *Konuşan adam susacak*, The man who-is-speaking will-be-silent.
> *Konuşan adam sustu*, The man who-was-speaking was-silent.

74

Like most adjectives, the present participle may be used as a noun: instead of *bunu bilen adamlar*, ' men who-know this ', we may say *bunu bilenler*, ' those who know this '.

122. Past Participle

*-miş*⁴ suffixed to verb-stem: *olmuş*, ' having been, who or which has been '; *olmamış*, ' who has not been '; *yürümüş*, ' who or which has walked '; *yürümemiş*, ' who or which has not walked '.

The English future perfect tense—' I shall have gone '—is translated by the past participle plus the future of *olmak*: *gitmiş olacağım* (' having-gone I-shall-be ').

123. Future Participle and Aorist Participle

These are identical with the future and aorist bases (§§ 102, 105, 106), which explains the use of the ' I am/was ' endings to form the future and aorist tenses: *gelecek* is a participle meaning ' about to come ', so *geleceksiniz* means ' you are about to come '; similarly, *gelir* is a participle meaning ' habitually coming ', while *gelmez* is a participle meaning ' not coming ', so *gelirsiniz, gelmezsiniz* mean ' you come ', ' you do not come '. It will be seen that although, e.g., *geleceksiniz* is conventionally called the future tense, the two elements composing it never lose their separate identities. ' I shall not come ' is *gelmiyeceğim*, but we may also say, with a rather different emphasis, *gelecek değilim*, ' I'm not going to come, I don't intend to come '. So with the negative aorist participle: *bilmez değilim* (' not-knowing I-am-not '), ' I am not ignorant '.

124. The Use of the Participles

It must be remembered that, while verbs usually come at the end of the sentence, attributive adjectives always precede their noun—*kız güzel(dir)*, ' the girl is pretty ', but *güzel kız*, ' the pretty girl '. So *bu saat çalar*, ' this clock strikes ', but *bu çalar saat*, ' this striking clock '. *O sokak çıkmaz*, ' that street does-not-come-out ', but *o çıkmaz sokak* or simply *o çıkmaz*, ' that cul-de-sac '. *Zaman gelecek*, ' the time will come '; *gelecek zaman*, ' future time '.

To translate ' who (which) has been/will be ', the past or future participle respectively is usually followed by *olan*, ' who (which) is '.

> *gelen adam*, the man who is coming
> *gelmiş olan adam*, the man who has come
> *gelecek olan adam*, the man who is going to come

Examples:

> *memur meşgul(dür)*, the official is busy; *meşgul olan memur*, the official who is busy
>
> *ism-i Hikmet'tir*, his name is Hikmet; *ismi Hikmet olan kardeşim*, my brother, whose name is H. (his-name H. being)
>
> *Kore'den dönmüş olanlar*, those who have returned from Korea (... returned beings)
>
> *bizi Türkiye'ye götürecek olan uçak*, the aeroplane which is going to take us to Turkey
>
> *parası olmıyan bir genç*, a youth who has no money (his-money not-being)
>
> *çalışmıyan talebelerden*, from the students who-do-not-work; *çalışmıyanlardan*, from those who do not work
>
> *babası ölmüş olan çocuk*, the child whose father has died (who-is his-father-dead)

N.B. *gelecek hafta*, ' next week '; *geçen hafta*, ' last week ' (where one would expect the past participle, as in this next example): *geçmiş zaman*, ' past time '; *geçmişte* 'in the past '; *gelecekte*, ' in the future '.

125. INTERROGATIVES

Several of these have been noted already, but no harm will be done by recapitulating. *mi*[4] turns any preceding word into a question. *ne*, ' what ', figures in a good many interrogatives— *niçin* (for *ne için*), ' why? '; *nerede*, ' where? '; *nereye*, ' to where? '; *nereden*, ' from where? '; *nereli*, ' belonging to where? '; *neci*, ' of what profession? ' It is also compounded with—*kadar*, ' amount '; *zaman, vakit*, ' time '; *gibi*, ' like '; *cins*, ' genus '; *türlü*, ' sort '; *biçim*, ' shape '; *asıl*, ' origin '; thus:

> *ne kadar*, how much?
> *ne zaman, ne vakit*, when?
> *ne gibi, ne cins, ne türlü, ne biçim*, what sort of?
> *nasıl*, how? what kind of?
> *kim*, who?
> *hangi*, which?
> *kaç*, how many? (*followed by noun in singular*)

Kim may take any case-ending and also the plural suffix:

> *Kimi gördünüz?* Whom did you see?
> *Kimleri gördünüz?* What people did you see?

Bunu kimden aldınız? From-whom did you take this?
Şunu kime verdiniz? To-whom did you give that?
Bu şapka kimin? (This hat of-whom?) Whose is this hat?
Kiminle beraber geldi? Together with-whom did he come?

kim, hangi and *kaç* may take possessive suffixes : *kim-iniz?* ' who-of-you?' (' your-who?'); *hangi-miz?* ' which of us?' *Bu bavullar-ın kaç-ı sizin?* ' How many of these trunks are yours?' *Ay-ın kaç-ında?* ' On which day of the month?' (' of-the-month on-its-how-many?'); *hangileri,* more commonly *hangisi,* ' which of them?' (cf. § 72 (5): the question ' which?' presupposes more than one).

kaça and *kaçtan* (' to, from how much?') are both used for ' at what price?' as is *kaç paraya* (' for how much money?'). *Kilosu kaça?* (' its-kilo for-how-much '), ' How much is it per kilo?'

ne may take case- and plural-suffixes, though unlike *kim* it remains in the absolute form when object of a verb (just as in English: "who saw *whom?* ' but ' what did *what?*'). *Ne yaptınız?* ' What have you done?' *Ne-niz var?* ' What's up with you?' (' What have you?'). *Ne-m-e lâzım?* (' to-what-of-mine necessary?') or *Bana ne?* ' What's it got to do with me?' *Ne-ler gördük!* ' What things we've seen!' *Neden* and *neye* (also *niye*) are both used for ' why?' Sometimes *ne* itself may be translated ' why?'

Ne karışıyorsunuz? What are you interfering (for)?
Ne güzel! or *Ne kadar güzel!* How beautiful!
Ne güzel çiçekler! What beautiful flowers!

126. Postpositional Expressions

(1) We can express the sense of many English prepositions by a roundabout phrase :

(a) behind	(b) at the back of
during	in the course of
by	through the agency of

For almost all prepositions not already given, the Turkish equivalents follow the pattern of (b). ' Front ', for example, is *ön* :

Ön-üm-de durdu, he stopped in front of me (at-my-front).
Ön-ümüz-den geçtiler, they passed before us (by-way-of-our-front).

Ev-in önünde iki ağaç var, in front of the house (of-the-house at-its-front) there are two trees.

Bu nokta-yı göz önünde tutmak lâzım, it is necessary to keep this point before the eye.

It will be noted that in the third example, where a definite house is meant, ' house ' and ' front ' stand in the Possessive Relationship, while in the last example, where ' eye ' is meta-phorical, the relationship is Qualifying. This rule is not always followed; definite nouns do not always take the genitive suffix before a postpositional expression.

(2) As postpositions are mostly used after nouns, and to express ' place where ' more often than ' place whither ' or ' place whence ', each word in the following list is shown in the form in which it usually occurs, i.e., with the 3rd-person-possessive suffix and in the locative case, but it must be remembered that all are variable in person and case, as shown above.

> *ön,* front; . . . *önünde,* in front of, before
> *arka, art,* back; . . . *arkasında, ardında,* behind
> *iç,* interior; . . . *içinde,* inside
> *dış,* exterior; . . . *dışında,* outside
> *üst, üzer-,* top; . . . *üstünde, üzerinde,* above, over
> *alt (-tı),* underside; . . . *altında,* underneath
> *orta,* middle; . . . *ortasında,* in the middle of
> *ara,* interval; . . . *arasında,* between, among
> *yan,* side; . . . *yanında,* beside
> *karşı,* opposite side; . . . *karşısında,* against, face to face with
> *etrāf,* surroundings; . . . *etrafında,* around

(3) The following are mostly used with the case-endings shown:

> . . . *hakkında* (in his right), concerning, about
> . . . *tarafından* (from his side), by, through the agency of
> . . . *uğrunda, uğruna* (in/for his luck), for the sake of
> . . . *yüzünden* (from his cause), because of
> . . . *sayesinde* (in his shadow), thanks to
> . . . *yerine* (to his place), instead of
> . . . *boyunca* (in respect of its length, § 96 (3)), along, through-out

(4) Of the words in the list in (2), only *üzer-* is never used with-out a possessive suffix. All the rest may be used like any other

nouns or (except *etraf*), as adjectives: *dış ticāret*, ' external trade '. *üstü* is used in qualifying relationships to mean ' at the point of ':

> *akşam üstü*, at the coming of evening
> *yemek üstü*, just at dinner-time
> *suç* (guilt) *üstü*, red-handed, in the act

(5) Two nouns followed by *arasında* ' between ' are linked by *ile* :

> *köylü ile bey arasındaki münasebetler*, relations between villager and squire.

(6) *baş* ' head ' is used postpositionally to indicate proximity:

> *vazîfe başında*, on duty
> *iş başında*, at work, on the job
> *silâh başına*, to arms!
> *yanımda*, by my side
> *yanıbaşımda*, right by my side

N.B. *masa başında* means ' at/around the table ', *not* ' at the head of the table '.

(7) Note *leh* and *aleyh* (Arabic: ' for him ', ' against him '):

> *lehte/aleyhte olmak*, to be pro/contra
> *lehimde/aleyhimde söyledi*, he spoke for/against me

Note : It will be seen that these ' postpositional expressions ' are simply nouns: we single them out under this heading as equivalent to a large and common class of English words (prepositions), but from the point of view of grammatical analysis *vapurun içinde*, ' on the inside of the steamer ', is identical with *vapurun güvertesinde*, ' on the deck of the steamer '; no grammarian would call *güvertesi-* a postposition. Cf. § 97, *Note* (i).

127. *aşırı*

As a suffix, *aşırı* means ' beyond, at an interval of ':

> *denizaşırı*, overseas
> *günaşırı*, every other day
> *iki kapı aşırı* (beyond two doors), at the third door down
> *ev aşırı*, next door but one

Its original meaning is ' excessive(ly) '.

128. The Verb: Imperative

The imperative is the form of the verb used in giving orders— ' Go! ', ' Sit down! ' The 2nd person singular of the imperative is the verb-stem, positive or negative, to which -$(y)in^4$ or -$(y)iniz^4$ is added to make the plural, the longer form being the politer of the two. There is also a 3rd person imperative in -sin^4. This must not be confused with -*sin*, 'thou art', which is unaccented and is attached to a tense-base, never to the naked stem; e.g., *gel-ir-sin*, 'thou comest', *gel-ecek-sin*, 'thou wilt come', but *gelsin*, 'let him come'. The suffixes of the imperative constitute the Type III verb-endings (§ 66).

2nd sing.	*gel*		*gelme*		
2nd plural	*gelin*	}come!	*gelmeyin*	}don't come!	
2nd plural	*geliniz*		*gelmeyiniz*		
3rd sing.	*gelsin*, let him come		*gelmesin*, let him not come		
3rd plural	*gelsinler*, let them come		*gelmesinler*, let them not come		

2nd sing.	*ol*		*olma*		
2nd plural	*olun*	}be!	*olmayın*	}don't be!	
2nd plural	*olunuz*		*olmayınız*		
3rd sing.	*olsun*, let him be		*olmasın*, let him not be		
3rd plural	*olsunlar*, let them be		*olmasınlar*, let them not be		

The following expressions, containing the imperative of *olmak*, are common:

> *hamdolsun*, thank God! (let praise be!)
> *sağ ol*, be alive-and-well! }
> *eksik olma*, be-not wanting! } colloquial forms of thanks
> *geçmiş olsun*, let it be past! (*of illnesses, i.e.*, wish you/him better)
> *oh olsun*, serves you right! (let there be *oh—a sound indicating pleasure*)

Note: The rule given in § 88, *Note*, does not apply to the Imperative. *Başlayın!* 'Begin!'

Vocabulary 7

açık, open
-*e āit*, belonging to
Allah, God
Bulgar, Bulgar
çakı, penknife
-*e çarpmak*, collide with, strike
dakika, dakka, minute (of time)
dil, tongue, language

diş, tooth
dizi, file, row
duygu, feeling
elbette, of course, certainly
ey . . . !, O . . . !
geç, late; *geç kalmak*, to be late
geçit (-ti), mountain-pass, passage

genç, young
göstermek, to show
göz, eye
hasret (-ti), regret, longing
hız, speed; hızlı, speedy, quickly
ilelebet, for ever
ısırmak, to bite
İslâv, Slav
istihkâm, fortification
istiklâl (-li), independence
korumak, to protect
köy, village
manzara, view, aspect
masa, table
mevsim, season
muhâfaza etmek, to preserve

müdâfaa etmek, to defend
ölüm, death
parmak, finger
sâde, plain, simple, simply
(-e) sâhip, owner, possessor (of)
sır (-rrı), secret
sormak, to enquire-about; -e or -den sormak, to ask someone
şark, east
tabiî, natural(ly)
tepe, hill, peak
tugay, brigade
uzatmak, to reach, extend
vazîfe, duty
yaprak, leaf
yassı, flat, level

Exercise 7

(A) *Translate into English:* (1) Bulgarlar Türktür, bunları İslâv yapan dildir. (2) Bunu kimden (kime) sordunuz? (3) Fakat bu hasret sade geçmiş zamana ait olan bir duygu değildir. (4) O kitabı bana uzatınız. Hayır onu değil, şu rafın üstünde dur-an-ı istiyorum. (5) Arkadaşınız, şu dizide dur-an-lar-ın kaçıncı-sı-dır?—Altıncısı. (6) Bu mevsimde açıkta kal-an-ı Allah korusun. (7) Tugayımızda yedi tane Mehmet var, siz hangisini soruyorsunuz? (8) Ey Türk genç-liğ-i, birinci vazife-n Türk istiklâlini ve Türk Cumhuriyetini ilelebet muhafaza ve müdâfaa etmek-tir. (9) Beni burada bekleyin, beş dakikaya kadar gelirim. (10) On dakika içinde onunla senli benli konuşmağa başladık. (11) Arkadaşlarımı burada beklemek istiyorum; olur mu? (§ 107, *Note* (i))—Olur elbette, neden olmasın? (12) Gözünüze çarpan manzara, iki yassı tepenin arasındaki geçitiyle tabiî bir istihkâm manzarasıdır.

(B) *Translate into Turkish:* (1) The dog showed his teeth as if ('like') about-to-bite. (2) Don't walk so quickly. (3) Take these photographs and put them on top of my table. (4) They say of (§ 94, *Note* (iv)) the East, ' It possesses the secret of death.' (5) Open the leaves of the book with the penknife, not with the finger. (6) Which horse came first? (7) Thank God our work is going well. (8) Let him not be late, let him come early. (9) Does the villager who has not gone out of his village understand these problems?—He does not understand (them). (10) They live two doors away from us.

LESSON EIGHT

129. THE VERBAL NOUN

(1) Besides the infinitive in *-mek/-mak*, there are three other verbal nouns, ending in *-me/-ma*, *-(y)iş*[4] and *-meklik/-maklık*. These three may take any of the possessive or case-endings, whereas *-mek* never takes possessive endings or the suffix of the genitive case. The declension of *-(y)iş* and *-meklik* calls for no special comment. Here are the cases of the other two verbal nouns:

	gelmek	*gelme*	*bakmak*	*bakma*
Def. Obj. .	*gelmeği*	*gelmeyi*	*bakmağı*	*bakmayı*
Genitive .	—	*gelmenin*	—	*bakmanın*
Dative .	*gelmeğe*	{ *gelmeye* *gelmiye*	*bakmağa*	{ *bakmaya* *bakmıya*
Locative .	*gelmekte*	*geimede*	*bakmakta*	*bakmada*
Ablative .	*gelmekten*	*gelmeden*	*bakmaktan*	*bakmadan*

For the alternative forms of the dative of *-me/-ma*, see § 88, *Note*. In spoken Turkish *-maya* is used in preference to *-mağa* for the dative of the verbal noun of back-vowel verbs; in front-vowel verbs there is, of course, no difference of pronunciation between *-meğe* and *-meye*. As for the meanings: *gelmek*, *gelme* and *gelmeklik* all mean ' the act of coming ', while *geliş* means ' the act *or* manner of coming '.

As *gelmem*, ' my coming ', is identical with the first person singular of the negative aorist—' I do not come '—*gelmekliğim* is preferred where ambiguity might arise. Apart from this, the *-me* form is much the most used.

Remember that the syllable before the *negative -me/-ma* is accented, and distinguish carefully the following forms:

> *gelme*, *bakma*, don't come, don't look
> *gelme*, *bakma*, the act of coming, of looking
> *gel-me-me*, *bak-ma-ma*, the act of not-coming, of not-looking
> *gel-me-m-e*, *bak-ma-m-a*, to my coming, to my looking
> *gel-me-me-m-e*, *bak-ma-ma-m-a*, to my not-coming, not-looking

(2) In addition to the regular negatives in *-memek*, *-meme* and *-meyiş*, there are two other negative verbal nouns: (*a*) in *-mezlik* : e.g., from *anlaşmak*, ' to understand one another ', is formed *anlaşmazlık*, ' misunderstanding '; from *saldırmak*, ' to assault ', comes *saldırmazlık*, ' non-aggression '. (*b*) in *-memezlik* : from *saymak*, ' to count, esteem ', comes *saymamazlık*, ' disrespect '. See also § 176 (5).

130. THE USES OF THE VERBAL NOUN

Verbal nouns, like all other nouns, must have the case-endings appropriate to the context. The *-mek* infinitive generally remains in the absolute form when object of *istemek*, ' to want ', and *bilmek*, ' to know ': *yüzmek istiyorum*, ' I want to swim '; *yüzmek biliyorum*, ' I know (how) to swim ' (*je sais nager*). When a verbal noun is the object of a verb other than these two, it takes the def. obj. suffix:

>*yüzmeği* (*yüzmeyi*) *severim*, I love swimming
>*Adalara gitmeği* (*gitmeyi*) *düşünüyordum*, I was thinking-of going to the Islands
>*oraya uğramayı unuttum*, I forgot to call there

Some examples are given below of uses of the forms set out in § 129. Note particularly the following:

(*a*) The dative of *-mek* or *-me* expresses purpose:

>*dün onu görmeğe gittik*, we went to see him yesterday
>*sigara almağa gidiyorum*, I am going to buy cigarettes

(*b*) The locative of *-mek* is used together with the verb ' to be ' to mean ' is/was in-the-act-of . . .' or as a simple present or past tense: *gitmektedir*, ' he is going, he goes '; *söylemekte idi*, ' he was saying, he said '. This construction furnishes the present tense most common in newspaper language, e.g.:

>*Millî futbol takım-ımız şimdi Roma'da oynamaktadır*, Our national football-team is now playing in Rome.
>*Şimdi Roma'da oynamakta olan millî futbol takımımız*, Our . . . team which is now playing in Rome (in-the-act-of-playing being our team).

(*c*) *-me* with possessive suffixes expresses the object of an order, a request or a hope:

>*Bekle-me-niz-i rica ederim*, I request your waiting, I should like you to wait.

Oda-ya gir-me-m-i söyledi (he said my-entering . . .), He told me to enter the room.

Buraya gel-me-niz-i istiyorum, I want you to come here.

(*d*) Verbal nouns in *-me* are also used as adjectives:

yaz-, to write; *yazma kitaplar*, manuscript books

.dol-, to be filled; *dolma kalem*, fountain-pen

doğ-, to be born, *büyü-*, to grow up; *doğma büyüme İstanbul-lu-dur*, He's an Istanbul man, born and bred.

as-, to hang; *asma köprü*, suspension bridge

Examples:

Bunu söylemek-le fena mı etti? (by-saying this, bad did he do?), Did he do wrong in saying this?

Onu bekleme-nin fayda-sı yok (of-awaiting him its-use non-existent), There's no use in waiting for him.

genç olma-sı-na rağmen, in spite of his-being young

okuma kitab. (reading its-book), reading-book

bekleme salonu (waiting its-hall), waiting-room

yürüyüş, way of walking, gait

görüş, way of seeing, outlook

alışveriş (taking-giving), commerce

nine-m-in hatırla-yış-lar-ı, my grandmother's reminiscences

Note: From a few verbal nouns in *-iş* adjectives are formed by the addition of *-li* and *-siz* (§§ 86, 87): *göster-*, ' to show '; *gösteriş*, ' ostentation '; *gösterişli*, ' ostentatious '; *gösterişsiz*, ' unostentatious '; *elver-*, ' to be suitable '; *elverişli*, ' suitable '.

131. Indefinite Pronouns and Adjectives

It will be seen that several of the words given below incorporate the 3rd-person-possessive suffix, e.g., *bir-i*, ' one of them '. This may refer back to a previously mentioned class of people, as in *çocuklardan biri* (§ 100 (1)) or to a ' them ' as vague as the ' they ' of ' they say ': *biri geldi*, ' someone came '.

Note that *kim-i* and *çoğ-u* may be used adjectivally; the possessive suffix then loses its force: ' some, most ', not ' some of them, most of them '.

Remember the ' pronominal *n* ' (§ 71); e.g., ' to somebody ' is *bir-i-n-e*. The *ı* of *bazı* is not a suffix, as the accentuation shows.

The possessive suffix is doubled in *bir-i-si, kim-i-si, hep(-i-)si* and *şey-i-si*.

biri, birisi, one, someone

> *Biri bu yan-a gitti, biri şu yana*, One went this way (to this side), one that way.
>
> *Birisi geldi, sizi sordu*, Someone came (and) asked-for you.

biri may follow a singular noun in the genitive case:

> *Padışah-ın biri*, one of (the class of) Sultan, a certain Sultan
> *herif-in biri*, some bloke

öbür, ' the other ' (§ 37 (3)); *öbürü*, ' the other one ':

> *Şu iki adamdan biri kardeşiniz, öbürü (öbür adam) kim?* Of those two men, one is your brother; who is the other one?

diğer, başka, ' other '; *başka-sı, bir başkası*, ' another one, some-one else '; *başkaları*, ' some others ':

> *Ben bu haber-i başkasından aldım*, I received this news from someone else.

bazı, kim-i, kimisi, ' some, someone ': *bazı insanlar, kimi insanlar, bazıları*, ' some people '; *bazı-mız, kimimiz*, ' some of us '; *bazınız, kiminiz*, ' some of you ':

> *Kimi kahve sever, kimi çay*, some like coffee, some like tea.

çok, ' many, much '; *çoğ-u*, ' most of it, most of them, most '; *çoğ-umuz*, ' most of us '; *çoğu zaman*, ' most of the time '; *çoğu insanlar*, ' most people '.

biraz, ' a little '; *birkaç*, ' a few, several '; *birçok*, ' a good many, quite a lot of ':

> *Biraz şeker verir misiniz?* Will you give (me) a little sugar?
> *birkaç kitap*, a few books (cf. § 91 (2))
> *kitapların birkaçı*, a few of the books
> *birçok ev, birçok evler*, a good many houses

bütün, ' whole, all '; *bütün gün*, ' the whole day '; *bütün günler*, ' all the days '.

her, ' every '; *herkes*, ' everybody '; *hergün*, ' every day '; *heryerde*, ' everywhere '; *hervakit, herzaman*, ' always '; *herhangi*, ' any '.

her is also the equivalent of ' -*ever* ' in ' whoever, whenever ', etc. Cf. § 158 (7).

hep, ' all, wholly, always, entirely, still '; *hep-imiz*, ' all of us ';
hep-iniz, ' all of you '; *hepsi*, ' all of them/it, everybody ' :

> *Hasta nasıldır?—Hep öyle*, How's the patient?—Still the
> same (thus).

şey (' thing ') is used for ' what-do-you-call-it/him ' :

> *Şey-i gördük, arkadaşınızı*, We saw what-do-you-call-him;
> your friend.

With this word the 3rd-person-possessive suffix may be doubled:

> *Bu kapı-nın şeyisi nerede—anahtar-ı?* Where's the what-do-
> you-call-it of this door—its key?

birbir-i, ' one another '; *birbir-i-ni severler*, ' they love one
another '; *birbir-imiz-i severiz*, ' we love one another '; *birbir-iniz-i
seversiniz*, ' you love one another '.

132. ' self '

In addition to its adjectival use (§ 72, *Note*), *kendi* may take the
possessive suffixes to give the sense of ' myself, thyself ', etc. :

> *(Ben) kendi-m böyle düşünüyorum*, I myself think so.
> *Bunu kim kırdı?—(Siz) kendi-niz*, Who broke this?—You
> yourself.

The 3rd-person suffix *-si* is often omitted; ' him-, her- or itself ' is *kendisi* or *kendi*, the pronominal *n* being inserted before
case-endings with either form; e.g., ' to himself ' is *kendine* or
kendisine.

kendi(si) is often used simply for ' he, she, it '; compare the
stage Irish ' himself ' for ' he '.

The reflexive sense may be emphasized by repetition:

> *Kendi kendimi yaraladım*, I hurt myself.
> *Kendi kendini (kendisini) yaraladı*, He hurt himself.
> *Kendi kendilerini yaraladılar*, They hurt themselves.

kendi-liğ-i-nden, ' from his self-ness ' means ' spontaneously, of
his/its own accord '.

133. TELLING THE TIME

> *Saat kaç?* (' hour how-many? '), What's the time?
> *Saat bir* (hour one), One o'clock, or simply *bir*, One.
> *(Saat) üç buçuk*, Half-past three.

(*Saat*) *iki-yi on geçiyor* (ten is passing hour two), Ten past two.

(*Saat*) *yedi-yi çeyrek geçiyor*, Quarter past seven.

(*Saat*) *beşe yirmi var* (to hour five there is twenty), Twenty to five.

(*Saat*) *on bir-e çeyrek var*, Quarter to eleven.

Saat kaçta? At what time?

(*Saat*) *ikide*, At two o'clock.

(*Saat*) *üç buçukta*, At half-past three.

' At — minutes past/to the hour ' is expressed by an adverbial form of the verbs *geçmek*, ' to pass ', and *kalmak*, ' to remain ', the number of the hour being in the def. obj. or dative case respectively:

(*Saat*) *beş-i yirmi geçe* (twenty passing hour five), At twenty past five.

(*Saat*) *beş-e yirmi kala* (twenty remaining to five), At twenty to five.

Note : *sularında* (' in its waters'), ' round about '; *saat dokuz sularında*, ' round about 9 o'clock '; *sekiz, sekiz buçuk sularında geldi*, ' he came, round about eight or half past '.

Vocabulary 8

-*e alışık*, accustomed to
altın, gold
Anadolu, Anatolia
ayrı, separate
beis, harm
belli, evident, clear
cep, pocket
-*e çıkışmak*, to scold, tell off
çirkin, ugly
dedikodu, gossip
defa, kere, time, occasion
dikkat (-*ti*), attention, care
doğmak, to be born, rise (sun, etc.)
doktor, hekim, doctor
dönmek, to turn, return
edebiyat (-*tı*), literature

-*e engel olmak*, to be the obstacle to, prevent
Erzurum, Erzurum (city in eastern Anatolia)
hastabakıcı, nurse
ilâç, medicine, drug
-*e lâyık*, worthy of, to
mendil, handkerchief
Mustafa Kemal (-*li*), Name of the founder of the Republic, later surnamed *Atatürk* (-*kü*)
nâzır, minister
niyet (-*ti*), intention
nutuk (-*tku*), speech; *nutuk söylemek*, to make a speech
ricâ etmek, to request
sebep, cause, reason

sürmek, to last, take (time)
teşkil etmek, to constitute, form
Vahdettin, name of the last Sultan
-e varmak, to reach, arrive at
vatan, motherland

-den vazgeçmek, to give up, abandon the idea of
vesile, pretext, opportunity
yer, place
yetmek, to suffice

Exercise 8

(A) *Translate into English :* (1) Erzurum'a üç defa, üç-ünde de ayrı ayrı (§ 99 (2) (*a*)) yollardan gittim. (2) Şimdi giren kızlardan çoğu pek çirkin. (3) Bu sabah iki mendil aldım. Biri ceb-im-de, fakat öbürü ne oldu bilmiyorum. (4) Bu bahs-in üzerine dönmekte beis gör-me-dim. (5) Doktor, hastaları dolaştı; bir hasta-nın ilâc-ı-nı vakt-i-nde verme-yi unut-an hastabakıcıya çıkıştı. (6) Dedikodu dinlemeğe alışık değilim. (7) İstanbul'a gitmek niyetinde-yim. Siz de gitmek istiyor musunuz? (8) Ay doğuş-u-ndan insan yürüyüş-ü-nden belli olur. (9) Hem Vahdettin'in nazırları, hem Mustafa Kemal'in kendisi Anadolu'ya geçmek için vesile aramakta-dırlar.

(10) Bu vatan için neler yapmadık!
Kimimiz öldük, kimimiz nutuk söyledik.

(B) *Translate into Turkish :* (1) It's ten to eight; at ten to eight; it's a quarter past one; at a quarter past one; they come about nine or half past. (2) This work is worthy to hold (a) place in our literature. (3) I've given up the idea of going to Erzurum to-day. (4) I request that you listen to me with attention. (5) At this rate (' with this manner-of-walking ') we shall have reached their house before seven o'clock. (6) This money is not sufficient to buy a gold watch. (7) This job won't take five minutes. (8) Does this constitute (a) reason for your taking my car? (9) Who prevented your doing this job? (10) Men don't live to eat, they eat to live.

LESSON NINE

134. THE *imiş* FORM OF THE VERB ' to be '

imiş, to which may be added the Type I verb-endings with the exception of *dir*, means ' is said to be ' or ' was said to be '; its use shows that the speaker has no first-hand knowledge of what he is describing: *Kızı gayet güzel imiş*, ' His daughter is/was very beautiful, I'm told '.

Just as with *idim* (§ 82), the initial *i* may be dropped and the -*miş* used as a suffix, subject to the fourfold vowel-harmony: *Gayet güzel bir kızı varmış*, ' He has/had a very beautiful daughter, they say '. Like *idim* too, *imiş* is unaccented.

imiş may be used after any tense-base except the *di*-past, to indicate lack of first-hand knowledge:

> *Profesör yarın gelecekmiş*, The Professor's supposed to be coming to-morrow.
>
> *Tren-le gidiyormuşlar* (*gidiyorlarmış*), They're going by train, I'm told.

It may also follow the past participle (§ 122); if I hear that there is a rumour that I have gone to China, I may say *Ben Çin'e gitmiş imişim!* ' I'm supposed to have gone to China! ' (' I-am-according-to-hearsay having-gone . . .'). Note that in this construction the *imiş* is usually separate not suffixed, to avoid the ugly *gitmişmişim*.

-*miş* may be added to the present, aorist and future bases before *gibi*, ' like ', to convey a doubt of the reality of the action: *Ağlıyormuş gibi gözlerini siliyordu*, ' He was wiping his eyes as though he were crying '.

135. THE -*miş* TENSE OF OTHER VERBS

(1) -*miş*[4] has a different force when attached to the stems of verbs other than ' to be '. Besides forming the past participle (§ 122), it is the sign of a tense which is sometimes called the narrative past, but which in this book will be called the *miş*-past. It differs from the *di*-past in that in the 3rd person usually (but see (2) below), sometimes also in the 1st and 2nd persons, it

90

implies a lack of positive knowledge. It differs from the *imiş* form of ' to be ': (*a*) in being exclusively a past and never a present tense; (*b*) in that *imiş* invariably implies a lack of positive knowledge.

> *gelmişim*, (I gather that) I have come, came
> *gelmişsin*, (I gather that) thou hast come, came
> *gelmiş*, I gather that he has come, came
> *gelmiştir*, he has come, came
> *gelmişiz*, (I gather that) we have come, came
> *gelmişsiniz*, (I gather that) you have come, came
> *gelmişler*, I gather that they have come, came
> *gelmişlerdir*, they have come, came

The *s* of the 2nd person is often dropped in pronunciation: *gelmişin, gelmişiniz*.

(2) The addition of *-dir* to the 3rd person in the written language removes the idea of uncertainty. *gelmiştir, gelmişlerdir* are the usual forms of the 3rd person past tense in newspaper Turkish: *General A. bugün şehrimize gelmiştir*, ' General A. came to our city to-day '.

Beginners tend to think that *-miştir* is used in newspapers out of modesty, in recognition that what a newspaper tells its readers is but hearsay. The wrongness of this belief is clear from the following considerations: (*a*) The past tense of ' to be ' in newspaper use is a self-confident *idi*, not a diffident *imiş*. (*b*) In headlines, where it is important to save space, the shorter *geldi* (for instance) is used, while the full text will have *gelmiştir*, synonymous but longer by four letters (similarly for the present tense the headline will have *geliyor* while the text has *gelmektedir*—§ 130 (*b*)). (*c*) It is only in the past tense that the *miş* appears; if the General's visit is to-morrow, the verb will be *gelecek(tir)*, not *gelecekmiş*.

(3) To summarise:

> *geldi* (written and spoken), he came, has come
> *gelmiş* (written and spoken), I gather that he's come
> *gelmiştir* (written), he came, has come
> *gelmiştir* (spoken), he must have come

The uncertainty implied in this last comes not from the *miş* but from the *dir* (§ 67 (3)).

(4) *dir* is sometimes added to the 1st and 2nd persons of the *miş*-past, to make a confident assertion of a fact not positively known (like a B.B.C. compère's ' Of course you all know our

guest-star '): *görmüşsünüzdür*, ' you have certainly seen, I expect you've seen '.

Note : In some districts of Eastern Anatolia, *-miş* and not *-di* is the usual base of the simple past tense.

136. THE PLUPERFECT TENSE

(1) We have seen how the ' I was ' endings are attached to the present, future and aorist bases, to make the equivalents of the English ' I was going, was about to go, used to go '. They may also be added to the *-miş* participle to give the equivalent of our ' I had gone ': *gitmiştim, gitmiştin, gitmişti, gitmiştik, gitmiştiniz, gitmiştiler* or *gitmişlerdi*. This tense has none of the uncertainty of the *miş*-past.

(2) There is a far less common pluperfect made from the *di*-past, in two possible ways:

(a) *gittiydim* (for *gitti idim*), I had gone
   gittiydin (for *gitti idin*), thou hadst gone
   gittiydi (for *gitti idi*), he had gone
   gittiydik (for *gitti idik*), we had gone
   gittiydiniz (for *gitti idiniz*), you had gone
   gittiydiler (for *gitti idiler*), they had gone

(b) *gittimdi* (for *gittim idi*), I had gone
   gittindi (for *gittin idi*), thou hadst gone
   gittiydi (for *gitti idi*), he had gone
   gittikti (for *gittik idi*), we had gone
   gittinizdi (for *gittiniz idi*), you had gone
   gittilerdi (for *gittiler idi*), they had gone

The pluperfect is used much more frequently than in English to show that one action in the past preceded another action in the past: see, e.g., Exercise 14, sentence 11.

137. THE PASSIVE AND THE REFLEXIVE VERB

A verb is said to be passive when the subject does not act but is acted upon. Active: ' The missionary ate.' Passive: ' The missionary was eaten.'

A reflexive verb is one whose action does not affect any external object but ' reflects ' back on to the subject: ' I washed myself.'

(1) Passive verbs are formed in Turkish as follows:

(*a*) to stems ending in any consonant but *l* the syllable *-il*⁴ is added;

(*b*) to stems ending in *l* the syllable *-in*[4] is added;
(*c*) to stems ending in a vowel, *-n* is added.

> *çekmek*, to pull, withdraw; *çekilmek*, to be pulled, withdrawn
> *tutmak*, to hold; *tutulmak*, to be held
> *yazmak*, to write; *yazılmak*, to be written
> *görmek*, to see; *görülmek*, to be seen
> *bulmak*, to find; *bulunmak*, to be found
> *almak*, to take, buy; *alınmak*, to be taken, bought
> *yıkamak*, to wash; *yıkanmak*, to be washed
> *söylemek*, to say; *söylenmek*, to be said
> *okumak*, to read; *okunmak*, to be read

(2) Reflexive verbs are formed as follows:

(*a*) to stems ending in a consonant the syllable *-in*[4] is added;
(*b*) to stems ending in a vowel, *-n* is added.

> *bulunmak*, to find oneself
> *çekinmek*, to withdraw oneself, refrain
> *yıkanmak*, to wash oneself
> *söylenmek*, to talk to oneself, mumble

(3) Comparison of the two preceding lists will show that, in verbs whose stems end in a vowel or *l*, the reflexive and passive forms are identical. Where confusion might arise, the passive is distinguished by a doubly passive suffix: *söyle-n-il-mek*, ' to be said ', while the reflexive sense may be unambiguously conveyed by the reflexive pronoun *kendi kendini* (§ 132).

(4) The passive of compound verbs formed with *etmek* is expressed either with the passive *ed-il-mek* or with a passive-looking form of *olmak : olunmak*. *tatbik etmek*, ' to apply '; *tatbik ediliyor* or *tatbik olunuyor*, ' it is being applied '.

The two common exceptions to this rule are *kaybetmek*, ' to lose ', passive *kaybolmak*, ' to be lost ', and *tıraş etmek*, ' to shave (someone) ', *tıraş olmak*, ' to be shaved, have a shave '.

(5) When a verb is made passive, the former object of the verb becomes its subject: ' I caught the ball '; ' the ball was caught '. In Turkish, intransitive verbs (§ 117) may be made passive; as there was no object to the active form, there can be no subject to the passive form, so such verbs are said to be used impersonally. Active: *istasyona bu yoldan giderler*, ' they go by this way to the station '; Passive: *istasyona bu yoldan gid-il-ir*, ' one may go by this way . . .' (' going-is-done '). This construction is the best

means of rendering the English indefinite 'one': *Kaç yaşında asker ol-un-ur?* 'At what age does one become a soldier?' ('. . . is-becoming-done?').

Reflexive verbs, too, may be used in the impersonal passive: *Burada yıka-n-ıl-maz* ('Here washing-oneself is not done'), 'One may not wash here'. Cf. § 150, *Note*.

(6) *başlamak*, 'to begin', is made passive when used with a passive verb: *rapor-u basmağa başladılar*, 'they have begun to print the report'; *rapor bas-ıl-mağa başla-n-dı*, 'the report has-been-begun to-be-printed'.

(7) *bulunmak*, 'to find oneself', is commonly used for 'to be': several examples will be found in subsequent exercises.

edinmek, reflexive of *etmek*, means 'to get, acquire'.

görünmek, reflexive of *görmek*, means 'to appear, seem'.

geçinmek (*geçmek*, 'to pass') means 'to live, get on (with some-one)'.

For the passive of *anlamak*, 'to understand', *anlaşılmak* is used.

(8) To indicate the agent of a passive verb, we may use the postposition *tarafından* (§ 126 (3)): *fincan, hizmetçi tarafından kır-ıl-dı*, 'the cup was-broken by the servant'. This use is not very frequent, because it is simpler to say *hizmetçi fincanı kırdı*, 'the servant broke the cup'. More common is the adverbial suffix *-ce* (§ 96 (3)). as in *Bu iş-e hükûmet-çe karar ver-il-miştir* ('to this work governmentally decision has-been-given'), 'This work has been decided on by the Government'.

138. As in English, names of materials may be used as adjectives or nouns:

> *gümüş-ten yap-ıl-mış bir saat*, a watch made from-silver; *bir gümüş saat*, a silver watch
>
> *mukavva-dan yapılmış bir kutu*, a box made from cardboard; *bir mukavva kutu*, a cardboard box

'Railway' is either *demiryolu*, 'iron its-road', or *demiryol*, 'iron road', the former being more common.

139. MONEY, WEIGHTS AND MEASURES

(1) One hundred *kuruş*, 'piastre', make a *lira*, 'pound' (approximately 10*d.*). The *kuruş* is subdivided into forty *para* (which also means 'money'), but as the *para* is now (1959) worth one-hundredth of a farthing, this unit is seldom met with.

The Italian lira is distinguished from the Turkish by being called *liret*. The English pound is *İngiliz lira-sı* or *isterlin*.

(2) The Metric system has been official in Turkey since 1932. Only those parts of it which are in common use are given below: just as in French 100 metres is theoretically *un hectomètre* but in practice *cent mètres*, so in Turkish *yüz metre* is far commoner than *bir hektometre*.

> *santimetre* or *santim*, centimetre—approx. $\frac{2}{5}$ inch
> *metre*, metre—approx. 39·37 inches
> *kilometre*, kilometre—approx. $\frac{5}{8}$ mile
> *gram*, gramme—approx. $\frac{1}{28}$ oz.
> *kilo*, *kilogram*, kilogramme—approx. 2·2 lb.
> *litre* or *kilo*, litre—approx. $1\frac{3}{4}$ pints

(3) There are two equivalents for ' square ' as in ' square kilometre '. The older method is to use the Arabic noun *murabbâ* (-*aı*—§ 48): *bir kilometre murabbaı* (' one kilometre its-square '). More frequent nowadays is *bir kilometre kare*. This apparent violation of the rule that adjectives precede their nouns is explained by the fact that the phrase has been lifted whole from the French *kilomètre carré*.

dönüm, formerly an area 40 paces by 40 paces, is now officially 1000 square metres.

(4) Two officially obsolete measures which one sometimes comes across are the *arşın*, a linear measure of about 28 inches, and the *okka*, a weight equal to a little over $2\frac{3}{4}$ lb.

Note: Remember to accentuate in pronunciation the first syllable of *metre*: *bir metresi* is ' a metre-of-it ', whereas *bir metresi* is ' a mistress-of-his ' (the French *maîtresse*).

140. ' A glass of water '

In expressions consisting of a number, a measure and the name of a commodity, such as ' a glass of water, a kilo of cheese, two packets of cigarettes, ten metres of curtaining-material ', the ' of ' is not translated: *bir bardak su, bir kilo peynir, iki paket sigara, on metre perdelik kumaş.* Compare the German *ein Glas Bier*, ' a glass (of) beer '. Note also the similar use of words meaning ' sort ': *bir yeni tip uçak*, ' a new type (of) aircraft '; *her çeşit insan*, ' every kind (of) man '.

The same construction is used with expressions formed with *dolu* ' full ', which with the 3rd-person-possessive suffix means

' -ful ' : *bir kaşık dolu-su şeker* (' a spoon its-full sugar '), ' a spoonful of sugar '. ' A handful ' is *avuç dolusu*, not *el . . .*, *avuç* being ' the hollow of the hand '.

141. THE LOCATIVE CASE

-de may usually be rendered ' at ', ' in ', or ' on '. It is also used with words denoting qualities, where we would use ' of ':

> *on bir metre uzun-luğ-unda bir ip*, a rope 11 metres long (in the length of . . .)
>
> *o kılık-ta bir adam*, a man *of* that aspect
>
> *bal reng-inde kumaş*, cloth *of* the colour of honey
>
> *güvercin yumurta-sı büyüklüğünde bir taş*, a stone *of* the size of a pigeon's egg.

Note : *Kaç yaşındasınız ?* ' How old are you?' (' in the age of how-many are you? ')—*Otuz yaşında-yım*, ' I'm thirty '.

Vocabulary 9

alay, regiment

albay, Colonel

ama, but

aralık, interval

ayrılmak, to be set apart, to depart

başarmak, to accomplish

boy, stature, length

çap (-pı), diameter, calibre

dāima, always

-e dāir, about, relating to

değnek, stick, rod

diken, thorn

emek, toil; *emekli*, pensioned, retired

emir (-mri), order, command

General (-li), General

gül, rose

hayli, pretty much, quite considerably

hemen, immediately

kalın, thick

kolay, easy

komutan, commander

konak, mansion, government house

Kore, Korea

kum, sand

lâkırdı, talk

müddet (-ti), period

parça, piece

pencere, window

savaş, war, fighting, combat

susmak, to be silent

-e şaşmak, to be surprised at

taraf, side

taş, stone

tercih etmek, to prefer

terfi etmek, to promote, to be promoted

tevkif etmek, to arrest

tören, ceremony

Tuğgeneral (-li), Brigadier

Ulus, ' The Nation ' (a newspaper)

uzun, long

üzmek, to distress, grieve
vilâyet (-ti), province *
yabancı, stranger, foreigner

yanyana, side by side
yazı, writing, article
yükselmek, to rise, ascend

Exercise 9

(A) *Translate into English :* (1) İki gün evvel Ulus'ta çıkan yazıyı okumuş olacaksınız. Okumuş ve şaşmışsınızdır. (2) Sus! Çocuğun yanında öyle lâkırdı söylenir mi? (3) Yeni yapılan vilâyet konağı, yakında büyük bir törenle açılacak. (4) On santim boyunda ve iki üç santim kalınlığında küçük bir değnek parçası. (5) Bir metre aralıkla yanyana duran iki taş. (6) Bu taşlar üzerine bir buçuk metre uzunluğunda bir iki santimetre çapında bir değnek konulur. (7) Yabancının hemen tevkif edilmesine dair emir almışlardı. (8) Siz portakalı seversiniz ama her halde böylesini yememişsinizdir. (9) Uzun müddet Kore Savaş Birliğimizin komutanlığını yapmış olan General Tahsin Yazıcı önümüzdeki ağustos ayında emekli-ye ayrılacaktır. Diğer taraftan, yine Kore Birliğimizin Alay komutanlığını yapmış olan Albay Celâl Dora da bu sene Tuğgeneralliğe terfi edecektir.

(B) *Translate into Turkish :* (1) I suppose I have always preferred the cinema to the theatre. (2) A day's train journey is covered ('is taken') in an hour and a half by aeroplane. (3) While I was looking out of the window last night, snow fell. (4) While I was sleeping last night, snow fell. (5) I hear you came to see me yesterday; I was very much distressed at (' to ') my not being at home. (6) They say the thornless rose does not occur. (7) You will be quite considerably tired. Because this is not a job which is easily accomplished. (8) The sand-hills here rose in some places to as much as sixty-nine metres. (9) Four times nine makes thirty-six. (10) Don't distress yourself.

* *Vilâyet*, the largest administrative division, governed by a *Vāli*. Each of its subdivisions is a *kazā*, governed by a *Kaymakam*. The new terms are *il*, *ilbay*, *ilçe* and *ilçebay* respectively.

D

LESSON TEN

142. The *dik* Past Participle

Besides the past participle in *-miş*, there is another, formed by adding *-dik*⁴ to the verb-stem, but in the absolute case this is little used except in some frozen forms.*

> *bir bildik, bir tanıdık*, an acquaintance
> *işit-il-me-dik*, unheard-of
> *gör-ül-me-dik* (not-seen), extraordinary
> *ol-ma-dık*, unprecedented

143. The Relative Participles

(1) The participles described in §§ 120–3 are used when in English the relative pronoun—'who, which, that'—is the *subject* of the relative sentence: 'the man who came, the light that failed, the train which will leave at noon'. In any other type of relative sentence—'the man whom we saw, the light which you switched on, the train he came on' (i.e., on which he came)—Turkish uses a construction which, though neat and logical, usually strikes English-speakers as one of the most alien features of the language. It will be dealt with at some length, as unless this construction is fully grasped it is scarcely possible to read a paragraph in Turkish.

(2) To the *-dik* and *-ecek* participles, a possessive suffix is added, to make a word meaning 'pertaining to my/thy/his, etc., doing. . . .' *-dik* is used for present as well as past time, *-ecek* for future time. Thus from *gelmek* :

> *geldiğim*, pertaining to my coming
> *geldiğin*, pertaining to thy coming
> *geldiği*, pertaining to his coming
> *geldiğimiz*, pertaining to our coming
> *geldiğiniz*, pertaining to your coming
> *geldikleri*, pertaining to their coming

---

* By 'frozen forms' is meant, e.g., such words as the English 'childhood, motherhood', the '-hood' of which is no longer a live suffix; we cannot say 'soldierhood' or 'scholarhood'.

geleceğim, geleceğin, geleceği, geleceğimiz, geleceğiniz, gelecekleri,
' pertaining to my, etc., future coming '.

Examples:

> *geldiğim tren* (train pertaining-to-my-coming), the train on
> which I came
>
> *alacağınız kitap* (book pertaining-to-your-future-buying),
> the book which you are going to buy
>
> *Oturduğunuz ev pahalı mı?* Is the house in-which-you-are-
> living expensive?
>
> *Herkes olduğu yerde kalsın,* Let everyone remain where he is
> (in the place pertaining-to-his-being).
>
> *Londra'ya gittiğimiz zaman kendisi hasta idi,* When we went
> (the time pertaining-to-our-going) to London, he was ill.

This last example shows the usual way of rendering ' when '-
clauses in Turkish.

The clumsy locution with ' pertaining to ' has been chosen as
being the only equivalent that fits all the examples. We may
memorize the translation ' which I gave ' for *verdiğim*, but this
will not work with intransitive verbs: ' the train which he came
(on), the place which I went (to) '. The beginner will therefore
be well advised to fix it in his memory that *-diğim* preceding a
noun means ' pertaining to my . . . ing '.

(3) Like any other word including a possessive suffix, the
relative participle may have a possessor expressed, in the genitive
case if definite: *mektub-u,* ' his letter '; *kardeşim-in mektub-u,* ' my
brother's letter '. So:

> *gönderdiği mektup,* the letter which he sent
> *kardeşimin gönderdiği mektup,* the letter which my brother
> sent (pertaining to his—my brother's—sending)
> *benim geldiğim gün,* the day *I* came

(4) If the subject is indefinite it remains in the absolute case:
Kedi bulun-ma-dığ-ı yerde fare baş kaldırır, ' In the place where there is no
cat (pertaining to its—cat—not being), the mouse raises (its) head '.

(5) *halde* is used after relative participles to mean either
' although ' or ' in a state of ':

> *bunu bildiğim halde,* although I knew/know this (in-the-state
> pertaining-to-my-knowing)
> *elinde bir bıçak olduğu halde,* having a knife in his hand (in-
> the-state pertaining-to-its—a knife—being in his hand)

(6) *yerde* after a future relative participle means 'instead of':
Evde bekliyeceğimiz yerde tiyatroya doğru yürümeğe başladık, ' Instead of
waiting at home we began to walk towards the theatre '.

Note: *geleceğim*, ' pertaining to my future coming ', may be
distinguished from *geleceğim*, ' I shall come ', by its position in the
sentence; cf. § 124. They are also accented differently; the
possessive *-im* of the former carries the accent, while in the latter
the *-im* is ' I am ', and the accent precedes it.

144. Like other adjectives, relative participles may be used as
nouns. This use is a grammatical device for making noun-clauses;
for attaching to a verbal notion the case-suffixes and postpositions
used after nouns. Its commonest function is to express indirect
speech, by putting a verb into the def. obj. case as object of
another verb, e.g., ' to say, to hear, to know ':

> *geldiniz*, you came; *geldiğiniz-i söyledi*, He said that you
> came (he stated the-fact-of-your-coming).

Examples:

(a) Genitive case: *gelecek-leri-nin müjde-si* (' of-their-being-
about-to-come its-good-news '), ' the good news that they will be
coming '.

(b) Dative case: *işit-tiğ-im-e göre* (' according to-my-hearing '),
' according to what I heard '.

The dative of the future relative participle means ' instead of ':
oraya gideceğime buraya geldim, ' instead of going there I came here '.
Cf. § 143 (6).

(c) Locative case:

> *geldiğimiz-de*, at-our-coming, when we came
> *çalış-acağ-ınız-da şüphe-m yok* (in-your-future-working my-
> doubt non-existent), I have no doubt that you will work.

(d) Ablative case:

> *Siz-i ara-dığ-ından haberiniz yok mu?* Don't you know he's
> looking-for you? (haven't you news of-his seeking you;
> cf. § 100 (1)).
> *zengin ol-ma-dığ-ından*, because he's not rich (from-his-not-
> being . . .)
> *Geldiğinden beri hastanede yatıyor*, Since he came he's been
> lying in hospital.

(e) with *için* ' for, because of ': *Doğru-yu söylediğim için kızdı*,
'He was angry because I told the truth '.

(*f*) with *gibi*, 'like'; *bildiğiniz gibi*, 'as you know': *Haber-i al-dığ-ı gibi yola çıktı*, 'Just as he received the news he set out (to the road)'.

(*g*) with *kadar*, 'as much as': *istediğin kadar al*, 'take as much as you want'.

145. NEGATIVE SENTENCES

kimse, 'someone, person', in negative sentences means 'no-body':

> *kimse gelmiyor*, nobody is coming (exactly like the French *personne ne vient*)
>
> *kimse-si yok*, he has nobody

bir şey, 'a thing, anything', is similarly used to mean 'nothing': *bir şey değil*, 'it is nothing' (used in reply to *teşekkür ederim*, 'thank you').

bir türlü, 'a sort', in negative sentences means 'in no way, no-how': *bir türlü anlamadı*, 'he didn't understand at all'.

hiç : (*a*) strengthens negatives. It is written as one word with a following *bir* :

> *hiçbir şey istemem*, I want nothing at all
>
> *hiçbir yer-e gitmezler*, they go nowhere
>
> *hiçbir vakit (zaman) gelmezsiniz*, you never come

(*b*) 'nothing':

> *Ne gördünüz?—Hiç*, What did you see?—Nothing.
>
> *bir hiç için kızdı*, he got angry for (a) nothing

(*c*) 'ever, never' in questions: *Hiç Konya'ya gittiniz mi?*, 'Have you ever/never been to Konya?'

ne ... ne ..., 'neither ... nor ...': *Ne onu gördüm ne başkasını*, 'I saw neither him nor anybody else'.

yok colloquially means not only 'there isn't' but also 'certainly not!' It is also used for 'not at home': *siz yok-ken kardeşiniz geldi*, 'while you were out your brother came'.

Note : Turks do not shake their heads to express negation; the conversational Turkish for 'no' is any or all of the three following: (*a*) a slight raising of the head; (*b*) closing the eyes; (*c*) the click-ing of the tongue with which we indicate mild vexation and which we write 'tut!'

146. TRANSLATION OF ' can '

-(y)ebil/-(y)abil- added to verb-stems expresses potentiality:

> *gelmek*, to come; *gel-ebil-mek*, to be able to come
> *geldiniz*, you came; *gelebildiniz*, you were able to come
> *söyle-n-ir*, it is said; *söylen-ebil-ir*, it can be said
> *oku-yacak mısınız?* are you going to read?; *oku-yabil-ecek misiniz?* are you going to be able to read?
> *görenler*, those who see; *gör-ebil-en-ler*, those who can see
> *oku-duğ-um yazı*, the writing which I read; *oku-yabil-diğ-im yazı*, the writing which I was/am able to read

Note (i) : It is possible, though rare, for negative stems to be followed by this suffix: *yaz-mı-yabil-ir-im,* ' I am able not to write ', i.e., I'm not obliged to write if I don't want to.

Note (ii) : The resemblance to our word ' able ' is a useful aid to the memory, but is sheer coincidence; the *-bil* is the stem of the verb meaning ' to know '; hence the lack of vowel-harmony.

147. TRANSLATION OF ' cannot '

The *-ebil* suffix is not used for ' cannot '; instead, an accented *-e/-a* is inserted before the negative *-me/-ma :*

> *ver-me-mek*, not to give; *ver-e-me-mek*, to be unable to give
> *kullan-ıl-mı-yacak*, it will not be used; *kullan-ıl-a-mı-yacak*, it will not be able to be used
> *almaz*, he does not take; *al-a-maz*, he cannot take
> *olmaz*, it does not occur; *ol-a-maz*, it cannot occur, be
> *tut-ul-ma-dı*, it was not held; *tut-ul-a-ma-dı*, it could not be held
> *başla-mı-yor mu?* isn't he beginning?; *başlı-ya-mı-yor mu?* Can't he begin?
> *yap-ma-dığ-ım bir şey*, a thing I did not do; *yap-a-ma-dığ-ım bir şey*, a thing I could not do

148. ADVERBS OF PLACE

(1) *içeri*, inside
   dışarı, outside
   yukarı, up, upstairs
   aşağı, down, downstairs
   ileri, forward
   geri, back, backward, behind
   öte, on the farther side, yonder
   beri, on *or* to the side nearer the speaker, hither

(2) When indicating motion towards a direction, these may be used just like their English equivalents:

> *kapıcı içeri gitti*, the porter went inside
> *aşağı geldi*, he came downstairs
> *geri döndük*, we turned back
> *beri geliniz*, come over here

They may also take the dative suffix (whereas the words listed in § 97 *must* take it when indicating motion towards) with no difference of meaning: *içeriye gitti, aşağıya geldi, geriye döndük, beriye geliniz*. For ' to the farther side ', the usual form is *öteye* not *öte*.

(3) When the locative or ablative suffixes are added, the final vowel of *içeri, dışarı, yukarı* and *ileri* is often dropped:

> *içerde* or *içeride oturuyorduk*, we were sitting inside
> *dışardan* or *dışarıdan geldi*, he came from outside
> *yukarda* or *yukarıda kimse yok*, there's nobody upstairs
> *ilerde* or *ileride*, in the future, in front

(4) These words may be used adjectivally, although *iç* and *dış* are used in preference to *içeri* and *dışarı* for ' internal ' and ' external ':

> *yukarı kat*, the upper storey
> *su-yun beri/öte yakası*, the nearer/farther bank of the stream

N.B. *Saat beş dakika ileridir/geridir*, ' The clock is five minutes fast/slow '.

(5) They are also used as nouns:

> *ev-in içeri-si karanlık*, the inside of the house is dark
> *cephe-nin biraz geri-sinde durduk*, we stopped a little way behind the front (of-the-front a-little at-its-rear)

(6) The suffix *-ki* (§ 98) may be added directly to *öte* and *beri* and to the locative case of the others:

> *öteki bina*, that building which is over there, yonder building
> *yukardakiler*, those who are upstairs

(7) Note the following expressions:

> *aşağı yukarı* (down up), more or less, approximately
> *ötede beride dolaşmak*, to stroll around (there here)
> *öteberi almağa çıktım*, I went out to buy some odds and ends (that-this)
> *öteden beri* (§ 101), from of old

149. *üzere, üzre*, now replaced in its original sense of ' on ' by *üzerinde*, is used:

(1) With the relative participle to mean ' as ': *yukarda yazıldığı üzre*, ' as is written above '.

(2) With *-mek* to mean: (*a*) ' so as to, in order to '—*çocuklar okul-a gitmek üzere hazırlanıyorlar*, ' the children are-getting-ready to go to school '; (*b*) ' on condition that, with the proviso that '—*yarın geri vermek üzre bu kitabı alabilirsiniz*, ' you can take this book on condition that you give it back (' to give back ') to-morrow '; (*c*) ' on the point of '—*arkadaşınız gitmek üzeredir*, ' your friend is on the point of going '.

Note : olmak üzere, ' as being '; cf. *olarak*, § 162.

Vocabulary 10

âlem, world, state of life

ancak, only

av, hunt, quarry

Beyoğlu (-unu), modern residential and shopping quarter of Istanbul (' Pera ')

bir daha, once more

-e dalmak, to plunge, be lost in

dolmak, to be full

döviz, foreign exchange

eğlenmek, to amuse oneself

el, hand

elçi, envoy; *Büyük Elçi*, Ambassador

emniyet, confidence, security

fena, bad

giymek, to wear, put on (clothes)

gülünç, ridiculous

haber, news-item; *haberler*, news; *haber vermek*, to make known

harbiye, warfare

hayat (-tı : § 64), life

hükûmet, hükümet (-ti), government

kânun, law

kovalamak, to chase

kraliçe, kıraliçe, queen

kumaş, cloth, (woven) stuff

mahkeme, law-court

mâlûmât (-tı), information

mandıra, cow-shed

mevzû (-zuu), subject, topic

müstesnâ, excepted

resmî, official, formal

rivâyet (-ti), rumour

sâha, area, field

salon, hall, auditorium

seçmek, to choose, elect

sıralamak, to put in a row, line up

söz, word, statement; *sözcü*, spokesman

tahta, wood, wooden

taklit etmek, to imitate

tat, taste, flavour; *tatlı*, sweet, delightful

tetkik (-ki), scrutiny, study

tezat, contrast, incongruity

turist, tourist

ummak, hope, expect

yarmak, to split, break through

Exercise 10

(A) *Translate into English :* (1) İşin fenası şu idi : bu hayat bir daha dönmemek üzere kaybolmuştu. (2) Bu kanunsuzlukların hesab-ı sorulacağı bir günün geleceğinden korkmuyorlar mı? (3) Şehirde kullanılan ve köylünün ' hükûmet ayı ' dediği resmî on iki ayı köyde pek az kişi bilir. (4) Londra'da Harbiye Bakanlığı sözcüsü bu gibi haberlerin bir rivayetten ileri gitmediğini söylemiştir. . . . Amerikan Büyük Elçisi bu haberden malumâtı olmadığını söylemiştir. (5) Türkiye Güzellik Kraliçesi dün gece Atlas sinemasında seçildi. Sinema salonu erkenden (§ 100 (3)) dolmuştu. Birçok kimseler de dışarda seçmelere girecek olan güzelleri görmek üzere sırala-n-mışlardı. (6) Tetkik mevzuumuz (§ 75 (3)) olan köyler (elli beş kilometre kadar uzak olan bir tane-si müstesna olmak üzere) Ankara şehrinin etrafında 20–22 kilometrelik bir saha içindedirler. (7) Hayatımızın tezatlarından biri de Beyoğlu'nda yaşadığımız, eğlendiğimiz halde onu sevmemekliğimiz, ondan bahsetmeği gülünç bulmamızdır. (8) Bir takım kimseler ellerinde Türk parası olduğu halde İstanbul sokaklarında döviz avcılığı yapmakta ve turist kovalamaktadırlar.

(B) *Translate into Turkish :* (1) I had a lot of work last night, I was able to go to bed only at one o'clock. (2) Fly, birds! to the place where I was born. (3) The unexpected stone splits (the) head. (4) The inimitable thing in them was not what they wore but their manner-of-dressing-themselves. (5) I shall let you also know the day I am going to see him. (6) It is doubtful whether I shall go to-day (' my-future-going is doubtful '). (7) Those who do not think-about to-morrow from to-day, cannot look with confidence at the future. (8) I shall never forget this kindness (' goodness ') which you have done to me. (9) How (' from where ') do I know what sort of stuff you want? (10) He stopped on the wooden bridge where the road passed which went from the city to the cow-sheds . . . he awoke from the delightful state into which he had plunged. He was like a man not knowing what he did (or) what he was going to do.

LESSON ELEVEN

150. THE RECIPROCAL OR CO-OPERATIVE VERB

The addition of *-ş* to verb-stems ending in a vowel, *-iş*[4] to those ending in a consonant, often conveys that the action is performed by more than one agent, either in co-operation or in opposition:

> *sevmek*, to love; *sevişmek*, to love one another
> *oynamak*, to play; *oynaşmak*, to play together
> *çarpmak*, to hit; *çarpışmak*, to collide
> *dövmek*, to beat; *dövüşmek*, to fight one another
> *görmek*, to see; *görüşmek*, to see one another, have an interview, converse

Not all verbs in *ş* have this force; e.g., *gelişmek* is not ' to come together ' but ' to develop ', *yetişmek* is not ' to suffice one another ' but ' to grow up '. Often they have a reflexive sense: *karmak*, ' to mix '; *karışmak*, ' to mix oneself in, to interfere '.

Note : Reciprocal verbs may be used impersonally in the passive (§ 137 (5)): *Arkadaşla dövüş-ül-ür mü ?* (' is fighting-with-one another done with-the-friend ? '), ' Does one fight with friends ? '

151. THE CAUSATIVE VERB

' His eyebrows rose; he raised his eyebrows.' ' The tree fell; he felled the tree.' ' Raised ' and ' felled ' are causative verbs; he caused his eyebrows to rise, he caused the tree to fall.

(1) Most causative verbs in Turkish are formed by adding *-dir*[4] to the stem:

> *bilmek*, to know; *bildirmek*, to make known
> *ölmek*, to die; *öldürmek*, to kill
> *unutmak*, to forget; *unutturmak*, to cause to forget

(2) Stems of more than one syllable, ending in a vowel, add *-t*:

> *oku-mak*, to read; *oku-t-mak*, to cause to read, educate
> *anlamak*, to understand; *anlatmak*, to explain, narrate, tell

(3) Stems of more than one syllable, ending in *r* or *l*, often add *-t*:

oturmak, to sit; *oturtmak*, to seat
darılmak, to be cross; *darıltmak*, to annoy

(4) A few monosyllabic stems, mostly ending in *k*, add *-it⁴*:

korkmak, to fear; *korkutmak*, to frighten
akmak, to flow; *akıtmak*, to let flow

(5) About twenty monosyllabic stems (half of them ending in *ç* or *ş*) add *-ir⁴*:

pişmek, to cook (intransitive: *sebze pişiyor*, the vegetables are cooking); *pişirmek*, to cause to cook, to cook (transitive: *sebze-yi pişiriyor*, she-is-cooking the vegetables)
doğmak, to be born; *doğurmak*, to give birth to
bitmek, to come to an end; *bitirmek*, to bring to an end

The other common verbs of this class are:

batmak, to sink	*düşmek*, to fall
geçmek, to pass	*duymak*, to perceive
uçmak, to fly	*kaçmak*, to escape
içmek, to drink	*aşmak*, to pass over
yatmak, to lie down	*doymak*, to be satiated

(6) Three common verbs add *-er/ -ar*:

çıkmak, to go out; *çıkarmak*, to bring out, extract, expel
gitmek, to go; *gidermek*, to remove
kopmak, to break off, out (intransitive); *koparmak*, to break off (transitive), to cause to break out

(7) The following form their causative irregularly:

kalkmak, to rise, depart; *kaldırmak*, to raise, remove
görmek, to see; *göstermek*, to show (also *gördürmek*, see *Note* (i))
emmek, to suck; *emzirmek*, to suckle (also *emdirmek*, to cause to suck)

(8) The object of the simple verb remains as object of the causative, while the subject of the simple verb is put into the dative case:

daktilo mektub-u yazdı, the typist wrote the letter; *ben daktilo-ya mektub-u yaz-dır-dım*, I got the typist to write the letter (to-the-typist I-was-the-cause-of-writing)

Biz müze-yi gezdik, we went-round the museum; *Orhan biz-e müze-yi gezdirdi,* O. took us round the museum

iş-im-i yaptım, I did my job; *işimi siz-e yaptırdım,* I got you to do my job

But if the simple verb has no object, its subject becomes the object of the causative:

çocuklar park-ta geziyorlar, the children are going-round, going-for-a-walk, in the park; *çocuklar-ı parkta gezdiriyorlar,* they are taking the children for a walk in the park
otobüs hareket etti, the bus started; *şoför otobüs-ü hareket et-tir-di,* the driver started the bus

(9) As well as ' to make someone do something ', the causative verb may mean ' to let someone do something ', particularly in the negative: *onu söyle-t-mediler,* ' they didn't let her speak '. *kaç-ır-mak* (' to let escape ') is ' to miss ', e.g., a train.

(10) A causative verb may take an additional causative suffix:

et pişti, the meat cooked; *aşçı et-i piş-ir-di,* the cook cooked the meat; *ev hanımı et-i aşçı-ya piş-ir-t-ti,* the housewife made the cook cook the meat (was the cause—to the cook—of causing the meat to cook)
fare öldü, the mouse died; *ben fare-yi öl-dür-düm,* I killed the mouse (I caused-to-die); *karım bana fare-yi öl-dür-t-tü,* my wife made me kill the mouse (was the cause—to me —of causing the mouse to die)

Note (i) : *görmek* can mean not only ' to see ' but also ' to undergo, receive ' (*tahsil görmek,* ' to receive education, study ') and ' to see to, perform '. In this secondary sense the causative is *gördürmek* : *bu vazife-yi ben gördüm,* ' I saw to, performed, this duty ' ; *bu vazifeyi bana gördürdü,* ' he put this duty on to me '.

Note (ii) : Reflexive and reciprocal verbs may be made causative: *bulmak,* ' to find ' ; *bulunmak,* ' to find oneself, be ' ; *bulundurmak,* ' to cause to be, to keep '. *Bakan-la görüşmek istiyoruz,* ' We want to have an interview with the Minister ' ; *Bizi Bakanla görüş-tür-ebil-ir misiniz?* ' Can you fix us an interview with the Minister? ' (' can you make us, with the M., see one another? ') But see *Note (iv).*

Note (iii) : Passive verbs are not made causative, but causative verbs may be made passive: *öl-dür-ül-dü,* ' he was killed '.

Note (iv) : Not all verbs in *-ştir-* are reciprocal and causative;

some of them convey an intensification of the meaning of the simple verb: *sormak* ' to ask ', *soruşturmak,* ' to make enquiries'; *aramak* ' to seek ', *araştırmak,* ' to investigate, research'; *atmak,* ' to throw ', *atıştırmak,* ' to bolt (food), to knock back (drinks) '.

152. USES OF *demek*

(1) As we saw in § 144, indirect speech is rendered by the relative participle: *geldiğinizi söyledi,* ' he said that-you-had-come '. If the speaker's actual words are quoted, *demek* and not *söylemek* is used for ' to say '. If Osman says to you *Yarın gelmiyeceğim,* ' I shan't come to-morrow ', you may pass the information on in three ways:

(a) *Osman, yarın gelmiyeceğini söyledi* (O. stated his-not-being-about-to-come), Osman said that he wouldn't come to-morrow.
(b) *Osman ' yarın gelmiyeceğim ' dedi,* O. said, ' I shan't . . .'
(c) *Osman dedi ki ' yarın gelmiyeceğim ',* O. said (that), ' I shan't . . .'

It will be noticed that part of *demek* may either follow the quoted words (like our ' " I shan't come," said he ') or precede with *ki,* ' that '. In this construction (*c*) *ki* is not translated into English, so ' He said, " No " ' is *Dedi ki ' hayır ',* while ' " No," said he ' is ' *Hayır ' dedi.*

As the actual words of the speaker can be introduced only by part of *demek,* ' He shouted, " No " ', ' " Where? " he asked ' are rendered ' " No," saying he shouted ', ' " Where? " saying he asked '. ' Saying ' in such contexts is *diye,* an adverbial form like *geçe, kala* (§ 133; cf. § 88, *Note*). ' *Hayır ' diye haykırdı ; ' Nerede? ' diye sordu.* ' *Sigara içilmez ' diye bir levha,* ' A " No Smoking " sign ' (' cigarette is-not-smoked saying a board ').

(2) *diye* does not only introduce quotations; it is used to introduce *unspoken* thoughts too:

Onu gelecek diye bekliyorum (him ' he will come ' saying I am awaiting), I am awaiting him in the expectation that he will come.
Değişiklik olsun diye otobüsle geldik, For a change (' change let-there-be ' saying) we came by bus.
Âdet yerini bulsun diye . . . (' let custom find its place ' saying), As a matter of form, through force of custom.

Hence the common *Ne diye . . . ?* ('what saying?') 'with what unspoken thoughts, with what motive, what's the idea of . . . ?' *Ne diye sizi yolladılar?* 'What was their idea in sending you?' If a self-assertive citizen is told, on entering a railway-compartment, *Yer yok !* 'No room!' and at once notices a vacant seat, he may say *Ne diye yer yokmuş?* 'What do you mean, "No room"?' The *-muş* implies that there is no visual confirmation of the statement.

(3) *demek* is used with the 3rd person singular of any tense of *olmak* for 'to mean', but only when the subject is inanimate, a word or a concept:

> *Bu söz ne demek(tir) ?* (what is this word to say?), What does this word mean?
>
> *İngilizcede* 'army' *ordu demek(tir)*; 'armies' *de ordular demek olacak*, In-English, 'army' means *ordu* and 'armies' will mean (will be to say) *ordular*.
>
> *Bunun ne demek olduğunu anladınız mı?* Have you understood what this means?

With the usual conversational omission of *dir*, *demek* alone can be 'it means': *Demek siz gelmiyeceksiniz*, 'It means you won't be coming'.

When the subject of 'to mean' is a person, use *demek istemek*: *Ne demek istiyorsunuz?* 'What do you mean?'—exactly the French *Que voulez-vous dire?*

(4) *-e demek* is 'to call, to name': *Bu çiçeğ-e biz gül deriz; siz ona* 'rose' *dersiniz, değil mi?* 'We call this flower (' we say for this flower') *gül*; you call it "rose", don't you?'

-e demek can, of course, also be 'to say to': *Ahmed'e bir diyeceğiniz var mı?* 'Have you anything to say to Ahmet, any message for Ahmet?' (' . . . a that-you-will-say ').

(5) *derken*, literally 'while saying', is also used for 'and just at that moment': *Ben tıraş oluyordum ; derken misâfirler geldi*, 'Just as I was shaving, the guests arrived '.

153. TRANSLATION OF 'must'

'must, ought' is translated by:

(1) the addition of *-meli/-malı* to any verb-stem; simple, passive, reflexive, reciprocal or causative. The 'I am/was' endings are suffixed as required:

gitmeliyim, I must go, ought to go

gitmelisin, thou must go, ought to go

gitmeli(dir), he must go, ought to go

gitmeliyiz, we must go, ought to go

gitmelisiniz, you must go, ought to go

gitmeli(dir)ler, they must go, ought to go

gitmemeliyim, I must not go

gitmemelisin, thou must not go

gitmemeli(dir), he must not go

gitmemeliyiz, we must not go

gitmemelisiniz, you must not go

gitmemeli(dir)ler, they must not go

gitmeli idim (gitmeliydim), I ought to have gone, I had to go

gitmeli idin (gitmeliydin), thou ought to have gone, thou hadst to go etc.

Note: The 3rd singular *gitmeli* means not only ' he must go ' but also impersonally ' one must go, it is necessary to go '. *Bir şey-i iyice düşünmeli, ondan sonra söylemeli*, ' One-must-think-about a thing thoroughly, after that one-must speak '.

(2) *lâzım* or *gerek*, ' necessary ', used with a verbal noun:

iyi düşünmek gerek, it is necessary to think well

iyi düşün-me-miz lâzım, we must think well (our-thinking well is necessary)

tıraş olma-m lâzım, I must shave

154. ' so-and-so '

(1) *falan, filân, falanca* all mean ' so-and-so, such-and-such ':

Ben falan oğlu falanım diye anlatmağa başladı, He began to explain (saying): ' I am so-and-so, son of so-and-so '.

Filân tarihte falanca geldi, On such-and-such a date, so-and-so came.

(2) *falan* and *filân* also mean ' and so on, and all that ':

Toplantı-da çocuk falan bulunmasın, At the meeting let there be no children and so on (i.e., babies, dogs, giggling girls and other nuisances).

Para falan istemiyorum, I'm not asking-for money or anything like that.

Mart-ta falan gelecekmiş, He's supposed to be coming in March or thereabouts.

(3) Another equivalent of 'and all that', very common colloquially, is made by repeating the word in question but with *m* substituted for the initial consonant or preceding the initial vowel: *Burada kutu yok*, ' There's no box here '; *Burada kutu mutu yok*, ' There's no box or chest or case or carton or anything of the kind here '. In the first example in (2) above, one could say *çocuk mocuk* instead of *çocuk falan*. *Arkadaş markadaş, herkes borcunu vermelidir*, ' Friend, relative, it doesn't matter who it is, everyone must pay his debt '.

If the original word begins with *m*, however, *falan* or *filân* must be used: *Mektup falan geldi mi?*, ' Have any letters or postcards or parcels or anything like that come? '

Note : falanıncı (§ 110) is sometimes used for ' the so-manyeth ': *falanıncı ev-in falanıncı kat-ında oturuyorum diye yazınız*, ' Write (saying) " I am living on floor number so-and-so of house number so-and-so "'.

155. The Suffix -*ip*

(1) When a Turkish sentence should contain a pair of verbs (the English equivalents being joined by ' and '), with the same subject and suffixes, differing only in their stems, it is usual to put the requisite suffixes only with the second stem and to add to the first stem the suffix (-*y*)*ip*[4]. Even if both verbs are negative, the first stem is left positive:

(a) *Oturabileceğiz*, We shall be able to sit.

(b) *Konuşabileceğiz*, We shall be able to talk.

(a + b) *Otur-up konuşabileceğiz*, We shall be able to sit and talk.

(a) *Cesaret-i-ni topla-dı*, He gathered his courage.

(b) *Sordu*, He asked.

(a + b) *Cesaretini topla-yıp sordu*, He plucked up his courage and asked.

(a) *Oku-malı-sınız*, You must read.

(b) *Anla-malı-sınız*, You must understand.

(a + b) *Oku-yup anlamalısınız*, You must read and understand.

gelip görür, he comes and sees

gelip görmez, he does not come and see

gelip göremez, he cannot come and see

gelip görmelidir, he must come and see

gelip görenler, those who come and see

gelip görünüz, come and see

(2) The Turkish way of saying ' I don't know whether he'll come or not ' is ' I don't know his-future-coming-and his-future-not-coming ', using *-ip*: *gelip gelmiyeceğini bilmiyorum*. Note that in this construction the negative does *not* also apply to the first verb.

Note (*i*): Though *-ip* connotes ' and ' in itself, it is often re-inforced by a following *de* (§ 95).

Note (*ii*): Do not use more than one *-ip* in a sentence.

Vocabulary 11

alıkomak, alıkoymak, to stop, detain, hold back

atlamak, to jump

batmak, to sink (intransitive), to set (sun, etc.)

beygir, horse

bitmek, to finish (intransitive), come to an end

bulaşık, infectious

delik, hole

deniz, sea; *denizaltı* (§ 78), submarine

er, private soldier

gazete, newspaper

-e gömmek, to bury, submerge in

hat (*-ttı*), line

hazır, present, ready

ısrar, insistence, persistence

-den ibāret, consisting (merely) of

-e ihtiyaç, need for, of

ilân (*-nı*), announcement, advertisement

inmek, to descend

işlemek, to work, function; *işletme,* causing-to-work, administration

karanlık, dark, darkness

kuduz, rabies, mad dog

kuvvet (*-ti*), power

makina, makine, machine, engine

manga, section (military)

marşandiz, goods train

mūteber, valid

muvāzene, balance, equilibrium

normal (*-li*), normal

Pastör, Pasteur

sağ, right

sefer, trip, voyage

sezmek, to discern, perceive

sol, left

telgraf, telegram, wireless message

top, ball, gun

virüs, virus

Exercise 11

(A) *Translate into English:* (1) Gece karanlığında yolcu tireni (treni) diye marşandiz-e binmişiz. (2) Topta bir delik olmalı, hep hava kaçırıyor. (3) Bu atla-yış ona muvazenesini kaybet-tir-di. (4) Demek kâğıt kalem falan filân alma-m lâzım. (5) Hazır bulunanlar bakıştı. (6) Bu içki içenlerin, yanındakilere de iç-ir-mek isteme-leri-nde-ki ısrar anlaşılır şey değildir. (7) Ahmet Mithat Efendi'ye, çok yazdığı için ' kırk beygir kuvvetinde bir makina ' derlermiş. (8) Gemiden alınan son telgrafta, geminin sulara gömülmeğe başladığı bildirilmekte idi. (9) Pastör, her bulaşık hastalığı doğuran bir virüs olduğu gibi kuduzun da bir virüs-ü olacağını sezmişti. (10) Deniz hatları işletmesi dün sebeb-i belli olmıyan bir emirle ' Seyyar ' vapurunu seferden alıkoymuştur. Vapur için sat-ıl-an biletler muteber olmak üzere ' Seyyar ' normal seferini cumartesi yapacaktır. (11) On dört erden ibaret birliğ-e manga derler. (12) Soldan değil, sağdan yürümelisiniz.

(B) *Translate into Turkish :* (1) The work finished yesterday; I finished the work yesterday. (2) We should have had an advertisement printed in the newspapers ('should have caused-to-print '). (3) Will you get that book down (' cause-to-descend ') from the shelf?—There's no book or anything resembling a book on the shelf. (4) ' What shall I do? ' I was thinking. (5) He's very formal with everybody. (6) That room over there is more spacious than this. (7) The submarine sank the ship. (8) I have come in order to learn whether or not you have need of me. (9) Come and see me to-morrow. (10) Will you wake me at half-past six?

LESSON TWELVE

156. Uses of the Future Participle

(1) In English we can say 'things to come', meaning things destined to come, and we can also say 'things to eat', meaning things destined not to eat but to be eaten. Turkish has a similar use of the active *-ecek* participle where one might expect a passive: *yiyecek şeyler*, 'things to eat'. Comparing § 143, we may regard *yiyecek* as meaning 'pertaining to future eating'.

> *Kaçacak zaman geldi mi?* Has the time come to run for it?
> (the time pertaining-to-fleeing).
>
> *Ne okuyacak kitap, ne de konuşacak arkadaşım vardı*, I had neither book to read nor friend to talk to.
>
> *Utanırım!—Allah Allah! Ne var utanacak?* I'm ashamed!—Good heavens! What's there to be ashamed of?

A common application of this principle is with *vaziyet* or *durum*, 'position': *Bunu yapacak vaziyette (durumda) değilsiniz*, 'You aren't in a position to do this' ('in the position pertaining to doing this').

(2) The future participle is used with *kadar* to mean 'enough to . . .':

> *ölüleri uyandıracak kadar gürültü*, noise enough to wake the dead (the amount pertaining to waking . . .)
>
> *cüce de-n-ecek kadar ufak yapı-lı bir ihtiyar*, an old man small-built enough to be called 'dwarf'

(3) *olacak*, 'which will be', is used to mean 'so-called, supposed to be': *Arkadaşım olacak adam beni yarı yolda bıraktı*, 'The man who's supposed to be my friend left me in the lurch ('at mid-way').

157. Translation of 'too'

The translation of 'too' is one of the commonest difficulties besetting the student of Turkish. The dictionary equivalent is *fazla* ('in excess') or *lüzumundan fazla* ('in excess of its necessity'). The fact that both words are of Arabic origin is an indication that we must look elsewhere for the natural Turkish equivalent.

(1) In such a sentence as ' I didn't buy it; it was too dear ',
' too ' should be translated simply by *çok*, ' very ', as the causal
connection between the two parts of the sentence is sufficiently
plain: *Onu almadım ; çok pahalı idi.*

(2) *fazla* may be used if the context is insufficient to convey the
sense of ' too ': *Babanız pek sabırlıdır.—Evet, belki biraz fazla
sabırlı,* ' Your father is very patient.—Yes, perhaps a little *too*
patient '.

(3) ' He was too tired to undress '; ' I am too busy to go to
the pictures '. For this type of sentence, Turkish uses the construction shown in § 156 (2): *Soyun-a-mı-yacak kadar yorgundu*
(' He was tired the amount pertaining-to-inability-to-undress ');
Sinemaya gidemiyecek kadar meşgulüm.

158. CONDITIONAL SENTENCES

Turkish has a special form of the verb for use where English
uses ' if '; it is *-se/-sa*, which like the *di*-past takes the Type II
endings. The conditional of ' to be ' is:

isem, if I am	*isek,* if we are
isen, if thou art	*iseniz,* if you are
ise, if he is	*iseler,* if they are

Alternatively, the endings may be suffixed; cf. § 82. Like *idi*
and *imiş, ise* is unaccented in all its persons, whether separate or
suffixed. *hazır iseniz* or *hazırsanız,* ' if you are ready '; *hazır
değil iseniz* or *hazır değilseniz,* ' if you are not ready '.

(1) Open conditions: ' if A, then B '.
Put *isem (-sem),* etc., after the base of the appropriate tense:

bilir-siniz, you know; *bilir-seniz,* if you know
çalışıyor, he is working; *çalışıyor-sa,* if he is working
içmeyiz, we don't drink; *içmez-sek,* if we don't drink
gelecek, he is going to come; *gelecek-se,* if he is going to come
verdi or *vermiştir,* he gave, has given; *verdi-yse* or *vermiş-se,*
    if he gave, has given

There are the same alternative ways of forming the conditional
of the *di*-past as of forming the *di*-pluperfect; *isem (-sem),* etc.,
may be substituted for the Type II endings, or *-se* may be suffixed
to them:

geldi isem (geldiysem) or *geldimse,* if I came, had come
geldi isen (geldiysen) or *geldinse,* if thou camest, hadst come

geldi ise (geldiyse), if he came, had come
geldi isek (geldiysek) or *geldikse*, if we came, had come
geldi iseniz (geldiyseniz) or *geldinizse*, if you came, had come
geldi iseler (geldiyseler) or *geldilerse*, if they came, had come

Examples:

Gelirsek mektubu getiririz, If we come we'll bring the letter.
Siz gitmezseniz biz gitmeyiz, If you don't go, we don't go.
Söyliyecekseniz (söyliyecek olursanız) söyleyin, If you're going to tell, tell.
Yemek yiyorsa dışarda bekleyin, If he's eating, wait outside.
Anlamadınızsa daha açık konuş-a-mam, If you haven't understood, I can't speak more openly.

(2) **Remote conditions:** ' if A should happen (but it's not very likely/frequent), then B would/will follow '.

For this type of sentence we use, not the conditional of ' to be ' attached to the appropriate tense-base of the required verb, but the conditional form of the verb itself, i.e., *-sem*, etc., attached to the verb-stem: *gelsem, gelsen,* etc. N.B. *isem,* ' if I am '; *olsam,* ' if I were, if I should be '.

Examples:

Ben sizin yerinizde olsam onlarla iyi geçinmeğe çalış-ır-dım, If I were in your place I should try to get-on well with them.
Siz olsanız ne yaparsınız?, If (it) were you what would you do? (' what do you do '; the aorist *yaparsınız* is more vivid than the past aorist *çalışırdım* in the previous example).
Haftalık toplantılara pek gelmiyor, gelse de soğuk duruyor, He doesn't come much to the weekly meetings, and if he does come he looks coldly on (stands cold).
Yarın gelsem olmaz mı? Won't it do if I come to-morrow?
Gitsem mi? Should I go?

(3) ' **Whether A or B happens, C follows.'**
The conditional of the verb is used, with *de/da* (§ 95) in both ' if '-clauses:

Yağmur yağsa da yağmasa da yola çıkmalısınız, Whether it rains or not, you ought to go out (both if it should rain and if it should not rain).

Biletçi ' Ayakta da olsan vereceksin. Otursan da vereceksin' dedi,
The conductor (' ticket-man ') said, ' If you're standing
(on foot) you'll pay, and if you're sitting down you'll
pay.'

(4) Unfulfilled conditions: ' if A happened/had happened
(but it doesn't/didn't), then B would follow/would have followed '.
The past conditional is used; this is formed by adding the *di*-
past of ' to be ' to the conditional base: *ol-sa-m*, ' if I should be ';
ol-sa-ydım (olsa idim), ' if I had been, if I were '.
Examples:

Elimde olmuş olsaydı buraya gelmezdim, If it had been (were
    having-been) in my hand(s), I shouldn't have come here.
*Herkes bunlar gibi düşün-se idi, şimdi hanginiz dünya-da olur-
    dunuz?* If everybody had thought like these people,
    which of you would be in the world now?

(5) ' If only. . .! ' Types 2 and 4 may express wishes, often
introduced by *keşki* or *keşke*:

Keşki gelseler ! If only they would come!
Keşke gelseydiler ! If only they came, had come!

(6) ' Although.' A conditional verb followed by *de/da* gives
the sense of ' although ':

Gittim-se de onu görmedim, Although I went I didn't see him.
Koşuyor-sa da geç kalacak, Although he's running, he's going
    to be late.

(7) ' Whoever, whenever, whatever.' Sentences introduced by
such words are treated as conditionals in Turkish. The relation
between the two ideas is seen in the English ' If anyone comes (or
' whoever comes '), say I'm out '; ' If I go anywhere (wherever
I go) he follows me '.

Her ne ister-se yapsın, Let him do whatever he wants (for
    her see § 131).
Siz ne kadar ez-il-iyor-sanız biz de o kadar eziliyor-uz, We're
    being squashed just as much as you are (whatever amount
    you are being squashed, we too are being squashed that
    amount).
Kim çalışırsa kazanır, Whoever works, wins.
Ne olursa olsun, Be it as it may (Let it be whatever it is).

(8) Conditional verb expressing commands. We sometimes use an ' if '-sentence to express a command or request: ' If you'll kindly step this way '. Turkish makes a similar use of the conditional verb, usually followed by an unaccented *e/a*, this being simply a vocative noise, like our ' Oh ' in ' Oh, do shut up!' *Otur-sanız a!* 'Do sit down!' *Dinle-seniz e,* 'Do listen!' (' Oh, if you'd listen.') *Baksan a!* 'Do look!' This may be impatient or courteous, according to the speaker's tone.

(9) Other types of conditional sentence. The two following examples illustrate two common ways of expressing an English ' if '-sentence. It will be noticed that neither contains a conditional verb. The first type is colloquial.

> *Ahmet değil de kim-dir?* If it isn't Ahmet, who *is* it? (It is not A. [all right then] and who is it?).
>
> *Orada bulmadılar mı buraya gelirler,* If they don't find it there, they come here (Have they not found there? They come here).

Note (i): *eğer* is sometimes used to introduce conditional verbs; it does not affect the translation: *(Eğer)hava güzel olursa gezmeğe çıkarız,* ' If the weather is fine we'll go out for a walk '.

Note (ii): Here are some common expressions containing a conditional verb: . . . *ise*, ' As for ': *Hikmet ise, pek tembeldir,* ' As for Hikmet, he's very lazy ' (' if-it-is H. [you're asking about] . . .'). *Ne ise,* 'Well, anyway '. *Nerede ise,* ' soon '. *Öyleyse (öyle ise),* ' if so, in that case '. *Hiç olmazsa,* ' At least ' (' if-it-is-not nothing '). *Zannedersem,* ' I think ' (parenthetic). *Bilse bilse o bilir,* ' If anyone knows, *he* will '. *Olsa gerek,* ' it must be ' (' if-it-be, then it is as it should be '). *Allāsen* (colloquial), ' For heaven's sake!' (for *Allahı seversen,* ' if-you-love God ').

Vocabulary 12

açılmak, to be opened, to clear (weather)	*gelin*, bride
-e alışmak, to grow accustomed to	*güç*, difficult
bağ, orchard, vineyard	*günah*, sin
çāre, remedy	*hâk (-ki)*, earth
dağ, mountain	*ihmal etmek*, to neglect
dert (-di), trouble, pain	*ilâve etmek*, to add
devir (-vri), period, epoch	*itimat (-dı)*, reliance
	kâfi, sufficient

(-e) *katlanmak*, to put up with, bring oneself to, resign oneself
keyif (-*yfi*), pleasure
kısım (-*smı*), portion
kötü, bad
Mısır, Egypt
okul, school

sayfa, page
saymak, to count, consider
Sultan, Sultan, ruler
toprak, earth, land, territory
yaş, age
(-*ile*) *yeksan*, level (with)
zahmet (-*ti*), trouble, bother

Exercise 12

(A) *Translate into English :* (1) Topraklarından büyük kısmı
denizaşırı bulunan İngiltere, denizi ihmal ed-e-miyecek vaziyet-
te-dir. (2) Ev-e yeni bir gelin geleceği zaman odalar kâfi
değilse eve yeni bir oda ilâve olunur. (3) Öğle-ye kadar hava
açılmazsa biz çıkmayız. (4) Eğer son sayfayı açıp okumak
zahmetine katlanırsa bunu görür. (5) Ötekiler olmasa bile sade
bu yeter. (6) Eğer bu keyfe alışmış olsaydım, tabiî ondan
vazgeçmek şimdi pek güç gelirdi. (7) Ne söylese dinliyen olmaz.
(8) Bu devrin eserleri, büyük bir itimada lâyık değillerse de,
yokluk içinde var sayılabilir. (9) Keşki gelip bana derdini
anlatsaydı . . . ben ona bir çare bul-ur-dum. (10) Şu muharebe
bitse de!—Ne olacak biterse? (11) Bak-ar-san bağ olur, bak-
maz-san dağ olur. (12)

Sev, seni seveni, hâk ile yeksan olsa;
Sevme, seni sevmiyeni, Mısırda sultan olsa.

(B) *Translate into Turkish :* (1) You are of the age to distinguish
good and bad. (2) Although I said ' I'm not going ', they
insisted. (3) If he doesn't know, let him ask. (4) As for my
brother, he never goes there. (5) If (only) they knew what sort
of man he is! (6) If he doesn't come by one o'clock, don't wait.
(7) Do be quiet! Do listen! (8) She does whatever she wishes.
(9) If anyone knows why Hasan hasn't come to school to-day,
Orhan will know; go ask him. (10) Come what may I must
finish this letter.

LESSON THIRTEEN

159. THE VERB: SUBJUNCTIVE

The subjunctive form of the verb expresses not actual happenings but wishes, concepts whose realization is desired. The base is -(y)e/-(y)a, to which the Type IV endings are added. The rule stated in § 88, *Note*, does not apply to the subjunctive.

> *ol-a-yım*, may I be, let me be, that I may be
> *ol-a-sın*, mayest thou be, that thou mayest be
> *ol-a*, may he be, that he may be
> *ol-a-lım*, may we be, let us be, that we may be
> *ol-a-sınız*, may you be, that you may be
> *ol-a-lar*, may they be, that they may be

So from *gelmek*: *geleyim, gelesin, gele, gelelim, gelesiniz, geleler*, ' may I, etc., come '.

Only the 1st persons, singular and plural (' I, we '), are in regular use. The 2nd persons are uncommon, while the 3rd survives only in a few stereotyped expressions (see *Note*). In place of the 3rd person subjunctive, the 3rd person of the imperative is used—*olsun, gelsin*.

In conversation, *ye/ya* is often dropped from the subjunctive of vowel-stems: *söyleyim* for *söyle-ye-yim*, ' let me say '; *başlayım* for *başla-ya-yım*, ' let me begin '. *Yapim* is often heard for *yap-a-yım*, ' let me do '. Note also *napalım?* for *ne yapalım?* ' what are we to do?'

The past subjunctive is formed, like the past conditional, by adding *idim*, etc., to the base:

> *olaydım, olaydın, olaydı, olaydık, olaydınız, olaydılar.*
> *geleydim, geleydin, geleydi, geleydik, geleydiniz, geleydiler.*

It is used for hopeless wishes, often prefixed by *keşki* or *keşke*; cf. § 158 (5). In this sense the conditional is more common in the spoken language. In Example 8 below we have the conditional and the subjunctive side by side, with no perceptible difference of meaning. Sometimes the subjunctive is used in ' if '-sentences; Example 9 shows how this comes about.

Examples:

(1) *Pencere-yi açayım mı?* May I open the window?

(2) *Lûtfen bir dakika bekleyiniz bir gazete alayım,* Please wait a minute (so) that I may buy a paper.

(3) *İster misiniz size de oku-ya-yım?* Do you want me to read to you? (Do you want I should . . .?)

(4) *Gidelim,* let's go; *bakalım,* let's look.

(5) *Biletsiz kal-mı-yalım!* (Let-us-not-remain ticket-less), Any more fares please?

(6) *Neresi ucuz ki orası pahalı olmasın?* What-place is cheap, that that-place should-not-be dear? (i.e., Of course it's dear; what place isn't?)

(7) *Karşındakini ne sanıyorsun?—Ne sanırsam sanayım!* (What do you think the-one-facing-you?—Whatever I think let-me-think), Who do you think you're talking to?—Never you mind what I think!

(8) *Keşke gel-me-ye-ydiniz. Yahut ki ben sizi gör-me-se-ydim!* Would that you had not come! Or that I had not seen you!

(9) *Bil-e-ydim buraya kadar gelmezdim,* If I'd only known (Would-that-I-had-known), I'd not have come this far (as-far-as to-here).

(10) *Oturdum ki biraz dinlen-e-yim* or *Biraz dinleneyim diye oturdum,* I sat down so that I might (may) rest a little.

(11) *Gelmediniz; bāri bir haber gönder-e-ydiniz,* You didn't come; you might at least have sent a message.

Note: *Allah vere,* 'God grant'; *Allah vere de yağmur yağmasa* ('May God give and if-only-it-doesn't-rain'), 'I hope to goodness it doesn't rain'. *Hayrola* (*Hayır ola,* 'may there be good'), 'Nothing wrong I hope?'

160. *Ki*

We have met this equivalent for 'that' in §§ 152, 159. It is written as a separate word, and in speech is never accented, thus being easily distinguishable from the suffix *-ki* (§ 98).

(1) *Bir adam ki nasihat dinlemez = Nasihat dinle-mi-yen bir adam,* 'a man that doesn't listen-to advice'.

(2) *Herkes bilir ki dünya yuvarlak-tır = dünya-nın yuvarlak olduğu-u-nu herkes bilir,* 'Everyone knows that the world is round'.

(3) *Öyle senli benli görüşüyorlardı ki görenler kırk yıllık ahbap sanırdı,*

'They were conversing so informally that the beholders thought (them) forty-year friend(s)'.

(4) Very often in sentences beginning with *öyle* or *o kadar*, 'so, so much', the explanatory words after *ki* are left to the imagination. *O kadar eğlendik ki!* 'We had so much fun that (I can't begin to tell you)!' The English idiom is to omit the 'that' as well. The film-title 'How Green Was My Valley' became in Turkish *Vadim o kadar yeşildi ki* ('My wadi was so green that . . .'). An intermediate stage may be seen in such a sentence as *Öyle bir sıcak oldu ki sormayın*, 'Such a heat happened that—don't ask!'; i.e., 'I can't begin to tell you how hot it was'.

(5) Note also these examples where *ki* is left hanging:

> *Dün tramvayda-yız. Hangi gün değiliz ki.* Yesterday we're *
> on the tram. Which day aren't we, that (I should
> single out yesterday?)'; i.e., 'as when are we not?
> *Bir kadın ses-i: Ne çekiyor-sun kol-um-u herif? . . . Sustum.
> Bana ne? Ben kimse-nin kolunu çekmedim ki.* A woman's
> voice: 'What are you pulling my arm for, scoundrel?' . . .
> I was silent. What was it to me? I didn't pull anyone's
> arm that (I should think she meant me).

161. POINTS OF THE COMPASS

The new terms are given in the left-hand column. Those on the right are the older terms, of Arabic origin, which are still current.

kuzey, North(ern)	*şimāl* (*-li*), North
güney, South(ern)	*cenūp* (*-bu*), South
doğu, East(ern)	*şark* (*-kı*), East
batı, West(ern)	*garp* (*-bı*), West

şimālî, northern
cenūbî, southern
şarkî, eastern
garbî, western

kuzey doğu, North-east, *şimāli şarkî*
güney doğu, South-east, *cenūbu şarkî*
güney batı, South-west, *cenūbu garbî*
kuzey batı, North-west, *şimāli garbî*

* Note the use of the present to make the narrative more vivid.

Note that the new terms are used both as nouns and as adjectives.
E.g., 'Western countries' may be: (a) *batı memleketler*, (b) *batı
memleketleri* ('west its-countries'), or (c) *garp memleketleri*.

162. ADVERBIAL FORMS OF THE VERB

The following suffixes, all subject to vowel harmony, are attached
to verb-stems, with *y* as buffer-letter after vowels.

(1) *-e . . . -e*

Denotes repeated action accompanying that of the main verb
and by the same subject. Usage requires a *pair* of verb-stems
when this suffix is used: *geçe*, *kala* and *diye* are exceptional (§§ 133,
152; see also 176 (3), (5), (7)). The accent is on the *-e* of the
first verb of the pair; for this and for the doubling cf. § 96 (2).

> *Bile bile yalan söyler*, He tells lies deliberately (knowingly).
> *Koşa koşa geldi*, He came a-running.
> *Sora sora aradığı yeri buldu*, With-constant-asking he found
> the place which-he-sought.

Instead of repeating the same stem, two different stems of
related meaning may be used: *Öksür-e aksır-a odama girdi*,
'Coughing and sneezing he entered my room'.

(2) *-erek*

Shows action accompanying or slightly preceding that of the
main verb. It is often interchangeable with *-e . . . -e*, but does
not connote *repeated* action:

> *Açlık grev-i yaparak öldü* (by-doing hunger its-strike he died),
> He died, having gone on hunger-strike.
> *İstemiyerek* or *İstemiye istemiye gitti*, Unwillingly he went.

The subject of the *-erek* is usually that of the main verb. The
chief exception is *olarak*, which may be translated 'as, as being,
for, by way of' or simply omitted in translation:

> *Türkiye'ye ilk defa olarak bin dokuz yüz kırk sekizde gittim*, I
> went to Turkey for ('it being') the first time in 1948.
> *Size şu kalemi hediye olarak veriyorum*, I am giving you that
> pen as a present.
> *Bana yol para-sı olarak on lira verdiler*, They gave me 10 liras
> for fare (being journey its-money).

A colloquial alternative is *-erekten*.

(3) *-ince*

Action just preceding that of the main verb: ' on doing . . .'
The subject may differ from that of the main verb:

> *Bahar gelince çiçekler açar*, At the coming of Spring, the
> flowers open.
> *Pencere-yi açıp Marmara'ya bak-ınca karşımda Adaları gördüm*,
> On opening the window and looking at (the Sea of)
> Marmara, I saw the Islands facing me.
> *Sizi görünce tanıdım*, I recognized you at sight (on-seeing).
> *Yüzbaşı ' nöbetçi nerede? ' diye sor-unca şaşırdım, burada
> olduğunu söyledim*, On the Captain's asking ' Where's the
> sentry? ' I was surprised (and) said he was here.
> *Sizden kitabı istemiştim, (siz) ver-me-yince bir tane satın aldım*, I
> had asked you for the book; you not giving (it) I bought
> one.
> *bana gelince* (coming to me), as for me

(4) *-inceye kadar* (*-inceye dek*)

' Until ':

> *Posta-cı gelinceye kadar bekledik*, We waited until the postman
> came.
> *Hava açılıncaya kadar yola çık-mı-yalım*, Let's not go out till
> the weather clears up.

(5) *-meden*

' Without, before ':

> *Size sormadan kaleminizi almıştım*, I had taken your pen
> without asking you.
> *Siz olmadan yapamayız*, We cannot do without you (you
> not-being).

The sense of ' before ' may be emphasized by adding *evvel* or *önce*:
Ben gelmeden üç gün evvel Konya'ya gitmiş, ' He went to K. three
days before I came '.

A less-common alternative form is *-mezden*.

Note: It is clear from the accentuation that the *-me-* is felt to
be the suffix of the negative, not of the verbal noun. Yet the
-den is felt to be the ablative suffix: hence the construction with
evvel, *önce* (§§ 101, 129).

(6) *-dikten sonra*

'After': *Mektub-u oku-duktan sonra geri verdim*, 'After reading the letter I gave (it) back'.

(7) *-eli (-eli beri, -eliden beri)*

'Since': *Buraya geleli hiç mektup yazmadım*, 'Since coming here I've written no letters at all'.

The subject of the 'since'-clause may be shown by inserting the requisite noun or pronoun: *Ben/Kız buraya geleli*, 'Since I/the girl came here'. Alternatively, the *di*-past may be used before the *-eli* form of the same verb:

> *buraya geldim geleli*, since I came here
> *oraya vardınız varalı*, since you arrived there
> *şu kapıdan çıktı çıkalı*, since she went out of that door

The negative verb with *-eli* is best translated as positive: *Oğlunuz maşallah* (§ 177) *biz görmiyeli çok büyümüş*, 'Your son has grown a lot since last we saw him' ('since we have not seen').

(8) *-dikçe*

Denotes 'all the time that . . .' or 'every time that . . .' The exact translation depends on the context:

> *İnsan yaşa-dıkça bilgisi art-ar*, So long as man lives, his knowledge increases.
> *Kız gül-dükçe yüzünde güller açılır ; ağla-dıkça gözlerinden inciler saçılırmış*, It is said that every time the girl laughs, roses bloom on her face; every time she weeps, pearls are scattered from her eyes.
> *Fil gibi, yedikçe yer*, Like the elephant, the more he eats, the more he eats.

Her 'every' is sometimes added: *Onu her gördükçe daha çok seviyorum*, 'The more I see him, the more I like him'.

> *gittikçe* (as it goes), gradually
> *oldukça*, rather, quite, quite a lot

(9) *-meksizin*

'Without': *Bir dakika bile kaybetmeksizin geldiler*, 'They came without losing even a minute'. *-meden* is commoner in this meaning.

(10) *-mektense*

' Rather than ': *Sinemaya gitmektense, burada oturup konuşalım,*
' Rather than go to the pictures, let's sit here and talk '.

Vocabulary 13

abla, elder sister
amma, but
Avrupa, Europe
boyun (-ynu), neck
bükmek, to bend
câmi (-mii), mosque
çabuk, quick
çeşme, fountain
dâhi, genius
-e devam etmek, to continue at, with
düğün, wedding
elbise, clothes
evlenmek, to get married
felâket, catastrophe
göçmek, to change one's abode, depart
güneş, sun
işte, behold, you see, there you are
itmek, to push

itiraz etmek, to raise objections
izin (-zni), leave, permission
kabul etmek, to accept
kader, destiny
kakmak, to push, prod
kalabalık, crowd
kâr, profit
kul, slave
lokma, morsel
meğerki (with subjunctive), unless
omuz, shoulder
sayıklamak, to rave about, talk in one's sleep
silkmek, to shake, shrug
sönmek, to be extinguished, go out (light)
Tanrı, God
yazı tura, heads (or) tails; *yazı tura atmak*, to toss a coin

Exercise 13

(A) *Translate into English* : (1) Metresi altmış dört kuruşa alınan bir kumaş-ı (§ 165 (1)) kaça satmalıdır ki her metresinde yüzde sekiz kâr bıraksın? (2) Bu iş bitmiyecek, meğerki siz de yardım ed-e-siniz. (3) Evlendik evleneli hiç sayıkladığını işitmedim. (4) Dünya dünya olalı son savaş (harp) kadar büyük felâket görmemiştir. (5) Başka elbise almıyayım demiştim amma şimdi işte arkadaşımın düğünü çıktı. (6) Kalabalığı ite kaka yarıp vapura bindik. (7) Ben bu dünyadan, dâhi'nin ne demek olduğunu öğrenmeden göçüp gideceğim. (8) Naim Efendi omuzlarını silkti ve ' ne yapalım, kader böyle imiş ' de-r gibi boynunu büktü. (9) Ablası Avrupa'dan döndükten sonra her şey değişmeğe

başladı. (10) Tanrı vermeyince kul ne yapabil-ir? (11) Ala-
cağınız radyo'yu yazı tura atarak seçmeyiniz! (12) Siz sigaranızı
iç-inceye kadar, ben yerinizi koru-r-um.

(B) *Translate into Turkish:* (1) So long as the sun is not extinguished, life will continue. (2) Istanbul is being gradually
left without trees. (3) I shall be able to read your article only
after finishing the work I have in hand (which-is-in-my-hand).
(4) Without eating a morsel of bread we had set out (had-gone-
out to-the-road). (5) Whenever the rain falls I always remember
that day. (6) One does not enter a house without obtaining
(taking) permission from-the-owner-of-it. (7) Some (as-much-as)
two hundred metres to (in) the west of the mosque there is a
newly built fountain. (8) Without raising objections he accepted
what I said. (9) It's turned (the hour has passed) half-past
seven; let's be quick; we'll be late. (10) Which day may I
come to you?

LESSON FOURTEEN

163. ADVERBS OF TIME

The English equivalents are italicized in the translation of the examples.

artık, ' at last, this is the turning-point, any more ':

> *Artık yaz geldi*, Summer has come *at last*.
> *Bıktım artık, I've-stood-it-a-long-time-but-now* I'm fed up.
> *Artık oraya gitmem*, I shan't go there *any more*.

daha, ' still, yet '; in negative sentences, ' not yet ':

> *Daha yatıyor mu?* Is he *still* lying in bed?
> *Mehmet daha burada mıdır?* Is M. *still* here?
> *Daha gitmedi mi?* Hasn't he gone *yet*?
> *Bir saat daha* (or *Daha bir saat*) *beklemeli*, It is necessary to wait one hour *more*.
> *Daha dün beraber oturup konuşuyorduk, Only* yesterday we were sitting and talking together.
> *Daha şimdi burada idi*, He was here *just* now.

hâlâ, ' yet ', may be substituted for *daha* in the first three examples. See § 12.

hemen, ' at once, just about ':

> *O girince hemen ayağa kalktılar*, As he entered they *at once* rose to their feet (to the foot).
> *Ben hemen o sıralarda gelmiştim*, I had come *just about* at that time.

In the latter sense, *hemen* is often doubled: *İşler hemen hemen bitmek üzere*, ' The work is *just about* on the point of finishing '.

henüz in positive sentences = ' just now, just '; in negative sentences = ' not yet '.

> *Henüz uykudan kalkmıştım*, I had *just* risen from sleep.
> *Dün gelmişler, ben kendilerini henüz görmedim*, They came yesterday (I'm told); I've not seen them *yet*.

yine, gene, ' again, still, yet '.   But in negative sentences ' again '
is *bir daha*:

> *yine gitsin,* let him go *again*
> *bir daha gitmesin,* let him not go *again*

arasıra, ' at intervals, now and then '.
bāzan, bāzen, kimi vakit, ' sometimes '.
bir an evvel, bir gün evvel, ' as soon as possible '.
bundan böyle, ' henceforth '.
dāima, her zaman, her vakit, ' always '.
demin, ' just a little while ago '.
derhal, ' immediately '.
ekseriyetle, ' usually '; *umumiyetle,* ' generally, as a rule '.
erken, ' early '; *geç,* ' late '; *ergeç,* ' sooner or later '.
ertesi gün, ' the following day '; *ertesi yıl,* ' the following year '.
evelsi gün, ' the day before yesterday '.
evvelâ, ilkin, ilkönce, ' first of all '.
geçen yıl, geçen sene, ' last year '.
gündüz, ' (in the) daytime '; *gecegündüz,* ' by day and by night '.
öbür gün, ' the other day '.
sık sık, ' very frequently '.
vaktiyle, ' formerly, at the right time '.
akşamleyin, ' in the evening '; *sabahleyin,* ' in the morning ';
geceleyin, ' at night '; *öğleyin,* ' at noon '.
akşamları, ' in the evenings '; *sabahları,* ' in the mornings '.
kışın, ' in winter '; *yazın,* ' in summer '; *(ilk)baharda,* ' in
spring '; *sonbaharda,* ' in autumn '.
Note (i): The *in* of *kışın, yazın* is not the genitive suffix but an
old instrumental case-ending.
Note (ii): *saat* (' hour ') also means ' point of time ': *O saat
geldi,* ' He came *at that moment* '.

164. THE SUFFIX *-cesine*

This extension of the adverbial *-ce* (§ 96 (3)) is mostly attached
to participles:

> *Vaka-yı kendi gözleriyle görmüşçesine anlattı,* He described the
> event as-if-having-seen with his own eyes.
> *El-im-i koparırcasına sıktı,* He squeezed my hand as-if-
> breaking-(it)-off.

165. *Bir*

(1) Nouns qualified by *bir* are not necessarily indefinite (§§ 56, 57): *Gözlerimle oturacak bir yer ara-r-ken arkadaşım bana boş kalan bir koltuğ-u gösterdi*, 'While I was looking round for (' while-seeking with-my-eyes ') a place to sit, my friend showed me an arm-chair (or 'seat in the stalls ') which remained vacant'. *yer* really is indefinite and remains in the absolute case, while the *koltuk*, being adequately defined, takes the definite object ending.

(2) The fact that *bir* may often be translated 'some, any '— *bir şey istiyor musunuz?* 'do you want anything? '—explains its use with plural nouns:

bir zamanlar (some times), formerly
bir şeyler mırıldanırlar, they mutter something(s)

(3) We say: 'Let's have a coffee '; 'Bring me a whisky-and-soda'. This construction is more widely used in Turkish: *Bana bir su (bir çay) getiriniz*, 'Bring me a (glass of) water ' (or 'of tea '). Cf. *bir şarapnel*, 'a (piece of) shrapnel ', in Military Extract 2, p. 160.

(4) As an adverb, it means 'only, once ':

Bir gördüğümü bir daha unutmam, What I have once seen I do not forget again.
Her haftada bir gelir, He comes once a week.
Her şey bitti, bir bu kaldı, Everything is finished, only this is left.

(5) *şöyle bir* means 'just a bit ':

Şöyle bir gez-ip geldik, We've just been for a bit of a stroll (We've just strolled and come).
Önce şöyle bir düşündü, sonra otur-up iki mektup yazdı, First he just thought a bit, then he sat down and wrote two letters.

(6) *birden*, 'all at one go ': *ilâc-ı birden içmelisiniz*, 'You must drink the medicine all at one go, at a draught '.

(7) Note also:

birdenbire, suddenly
ikide bir(de), frequently
bir varmış bir yokmuş, once upon a time (once there was and once there wasn't)

N.B. *iki günde bir*, 'Every *third* day '.

166. The 3rd-person-possessive Suffix

The student will by now have an idea of the enormous part played in Turkish by the suffix -(*s*)*i*. To summarize: it may relate the word to which it is attached (*a*) to a preceding word in the genitive case: *Bu kitab-ın bir nüsha-sı*, ' One copy of this book '; (*b*) to a preceding word in the absolute case: *Sovyet hükûmet-i*, ' The Soviet Government '; (*c*) to a word understood from the context but not expressed: *Müdür, oda-sı-nda-dır*, ' The Director is in his room ', i.e., *müdür-ün odasında*. *Bu söz yer-i-nde-dir*, ' This remark is appropriate ' (' in-its-place '). *Şu kumaş çok pahalı. Ondan daha ucuz-u yok mu?* ' That stuff is too dear. Isn't there any cheaper (of it)? ' Cf. *vaktinde*, Exercise 8, A. (5).

The antecedent may be quite vague (cf. *bir-i*, § 131); it may be the whole circumstances of an action:

> *İyi-si, hep beraber kalk-ıp oraya gidelim*, The best thing to do is (the-good-of-it), let's all get up and go there together.
> *Hâsıl-ı, ne yaptımsa fayda etmedi*, In short (the-result-of-it), whatever I did achieved nothing.
> *Fena-sı şu-dur ki . . .*, The worst part about it (the-bad-of-it) is this, that . . .
> *Doğru-su . . .* (' the-true-of-it '), To tell you the truth . . .
> *Daha doğrusu . . .*, To be more precise . . .
> *İcab-ı-nda . . .* (in-its-necessitating), If necessary . . . If need arises . . .
> *Daha acı-sı . . .* (the more-painful-of-it), Still more painful is the fact that . . .
> *Eski-si gibi . . .* (like the-old-of-it), As before, as of old . . .
> *Şura-sı da var . . .* (this-place-of-it also exists), There's this point about it too . . .
> *Ora-sı öyle* (that-place-of-it is thus), That's so.
> *İnad-ı-na* (for-the-obstinacy-of-it), Just to be awkward, Out of sheer cussedness.
> *Türkçesi . . .* (the-Turkish-of-it), In plain language . . ., To put it bluntly . . . (*Türkçesi, sen bu işi beceremedin*, To put it bluntly, you haven't handled this matter properly.)

167. Other Useful Adverbs, Conjunctions and Particles

âdetâ, ' virtually, simply, pretty well '.
âferin, ' Bravo! '

amma, ama, fakat, lâkin, ' but ' (*lâkin* is old-fashioned).
ancak, yalnız, ' only '. See *Note.*
aşkolsun, (a) ' Bravo! ' (*b*) ' It's too bad of you! '
bâri, hiç olmazsa, ' at least, at any rate '.
. . . *bile, hattâ* . . ., ' even ':

> *Beni bile aldattı,* He deceived even me.
> *Daha kalkmadı bile,* He hasn't even got up yet.
> *Hattâ gözümle görsem inanmam,* Even if I should see it with my (own) eye I shan't believe it.

For an example of *bile* and *hattâ* used together see Exercise 14, No. 18.

bilhassa, ' especially '.
dahi, ' also '.
elbet, elbette (both accented on first or second syllable), ' certainly '.
esâsen, zâten, ' essentially, as a matter of fact ': *Zahmet oldu de-me-yin, ben esasen gelecektim,* ' Don't say it was a bother; as a matter of fact I was coming anyway '.
eyvâh, ' Alas! Oh, dear! '
gerek . . . *gerek(se)* . . .; *hem* . . . *hem* . . ., ' both . . . and . . .'
hakikaten, gerçekten, sahiden, ' truly, really '.
ha? asks indignant questions: *Bizi görmeden gitti ha?* ' He's gone without seeing us, has he? '
hâlbuki, oysa ki, ' whereas '.
hani, haniya introduces questions about something expected which hasn't materialized or whose absence is regretted:

> *Haniya çamaşır-ım?* Where's my laundry then?
> *Hani gidiyordunuz?* I thought you were going?

haydi, ' Come on! '
hele, ' at least, just ': *Hele bak, neler söylüyor!* ' Just look, the things he's saying! '
hem, ' and, and indeed, in fact ': *Gidiyor, hem koşarak gidiyor,* ' He's going; in fact, he's going at the double '. *Hem de nasıl!* is exactly the American ' And how! '
imdat, ' Help! '
mâdem, mâdemki, ' since, inasmuch as '.
meğer, ' it turns out that . . .' (with *-miş,* § 134): *Meğer ben*

aldan-mış-ım, 'So I've been deceived!' Note also *meğerki,*
Exercise 13, A. (2).

meselâ, 'for example'.

mutlaka, 'absolutely, positively'.

neyse, ne ise, 'well, anyway'.

nitekim, nasıl ki, 'just as, in the same way as'.

pekâlâ, 'all right!' *Pekâlâ, madem biliyordunuz ne diye söyle-
mediniz?* 'All right, since you knew, what was the idea of not
saying?'

peki (for *pek iyi*), 'very good, very well'.

sahi? sahi mi? 'Really?'

sakın, 'Mind! Take care!'

sanki (san ki, 'suppose that'), 'As if, suppose':

> *Sanki sahiden öyle söylemişim, ne çıkar?* Suppose I really did
> say so, what of it? (what comes-out?).
> *Sanki ne olmuş?* What's supposed to have happened?
> *Sanki başka bir otel yokmuş gibi!* Anyone would think there
> wasn't another hotel! (Like as-if there wasn't . . .).

tabiî, 'naturally, of course'.

veya, yāhut, ya, 'or'.

ya has a large number of uses, the commonest of which may be
grouped thus: (*a*) 'yes indeed', (*b*) 'and what about . . .?'
(at the beginning of a clause), (*c*) 'isn't that so?'

Examples:

> (*a*) *O da gelmeli imiş.—Gelmeli ya!* They're saying he
> ought to have come too.—Yes indeed, so he ought!
> (*b*) *Siz konferans-a gidiyorsunuz, ya ben ne yapayım?* You're
> going to the lecture; and what about me, what am I to do?
> (*c*) *Hani meyva alacaktınız?—Dün aldım ya!* I thought you
> were going to buy some fruit?—Well I bought (some)
> yesterday, didn't I?

ya . . . ya . . . veya (yahut) . . ., 'Either . . . or . . . or . . .'

yāni, 'it means': *Gidecek misiniz yani?* 'It means you're going?'

yazık, 'what a pity.' *Yazıklar olsun!* 'Shame!'

yoksa ('if not'), 'otherwise, or'.

Note: yalnız, 'only', but *yalnız,* 'alone'; *yalnız başıma,* 'all
by myself'.

168. The Suffix -esi

-esi attached to verb stems is an old form of future tense. Its chief use nowadays is in cursing, sometimes with *-ce* added:

> *Kör olası(ca) !* May he become blind!
> *Ad-ı batası(ca) !* May his name sink!
> *İp-e gelesi(ce)*, May he come to the rope!

Such expressions also serve as adjectives—*kör olası herif!* ' The damned scoundrel! '—and nouns. *Adı batası*, in particular, is applied to diseases: *Çocuk bu adı batası-ya tutulmuş*, ' The child has caught this damnable-thing '.

169. The Suffix -daş

Denotes ' -fellow ': the vowel is invariable.

> *arka-daş* (back-fellow), friend
> *din-daş* (religion-fellow), co-religionist
> *meslek-taş* (profession-fellow), colleague
> *vatan-daş* (motherland-fellow), fellow-citizen

The non-harmonic *kardeş*, ' brother ', of Istanbul Turkish, is *kardaş* in local dialects; this for an earlier *karın-daş*, ' womb-fellow '.

' Namesake ' is *adaş*, though one would expect a double *d* (*ad* ' name ').

170. Diminutives

The following suffixes have the sense of ' little, dear little ', occasionally ' poor little ':

(1) *-cik* (this suffix throws the accent on to the first syllable):

> *ev-cik*, little house
> *anne-ciğ-im*, mummy
> *baba-cığ-ım*, daddy

Adjectives ending in *k* must, nouns ending in *k* may, drop the *k* before *-cik*:

> *ufak*, tiny; *ufa-cık*, tiny little
> *yumuşak*, soft; *yumuşa-cık bir yatak*, a lovely soft bed
> *bebek*, baby; *bebecik* (more rarely *bebekçik*), dear little baby
> *eşek*, donkey; *eşecik* or *eşekçik*, little donkey

With adverbs: *şimdi*, ' now ', *şimdicik* (colloquially *şimcik*),
' right now '; *bu kadarcık*, ' just this much, this small amount '.

az, ' little ', makes *azıcık* or *azcık*. *dar*, ' narrow ', *daracık*,
' rather narrow '. *bir*, ' one ', *biricik*, ' sole, only one, unique '.

(2) *-ce*, like our ' quite ', may increase as well as diminish the
force of the adjective or adverb to which it is attached: *iyi*, ' good,
well '; *iyice*, ' quite good, pretty well ' (distinguish from *iyice*,
' thoroughly '—§ 96 (3)); *seyrek*, ' wide apart; *seyrekçe*, ' rather
infrequent(ly) '.

(3) (1) and (2) may be combined: *yakın-ca-cık*, ' very near,
pretty close '.

(4) *-ceğiz*. Note especially *adamcağız*, usually pityingly, ' the
poor chap, the poor wee man '.

(5) *-(i)msi*, *-(i)mtrak*. These are mostly used with adjectives
of colour and equal our ' -ish '. The *a* of *-mtrak* (also spelled
-mtırak) is invariable, as a rule, though some people do subject
it to vowel harmony.

> *sarı*, yellow; *sarımsı*, *sarımtrak*, yellowish
> *beyaz*, white; *beyazımtrak*, *beyazımsı*, whitish
> *ekşi*, sour; *ekşimtrak*, *ekşimsi*, sourish
> *budala*, fool; *budalamsı*, foolish
> *argo*, slang, argot; *argomsu*, slangy, slangish

(6) *-si* is used with nouns and adjectives to mean ' -ish ':
çocuksu, ' childish '; *erkeksi*, ' mannish '; *yılansı*, ' snaky '; *yeşilsi*,
' greenish '.

171. The Suffix *-(y)ici*

This suffix, attached to verb-stems, denotes regular occupation,
habitual activity (cf. *-ci*, § 113): it may usually be rendered by
the English suffix ' -er ':

> *oku-mak*, to read; *oku-yucu*, reader
> *dinle-mek*, to listen; *sayın dinle-yici-ler*, honoured listeners
> *sat-mak*, to sell; *sokak sat-ıcı-sı*, street trader
> *hastabakıcı*, nurse (patient-looker)
> *haşerat öldür-ücü ilâç*, insecticide (insect killer drug)
> *kuvvet ver-ici*, bracing (strength giver)
> *gül-mek*, to laugh; *gül-dür-mek*, to make laugh; *gül-dür-*
> *ücü*, amusing

Vocabulary 14

-e bağlı, depending on
beslemek, to rear, nurture
biçmek, to cut out (clothes), to reap
bol, ample, abundant
burun (-rnu), nose
dâvet (-ti), invitation
fazla, excessive, superfluous
fiyat (-tı), fiat (-ti), price
hoca, teacher
hüzün (-znü), sadness
kavga etmek, to quarrel, have a row
kekre, sour, acrid
koğmak, kovmak (§ 19 (4)), to drive away, throw out

koyun (-ynu), chest, bosom
liyâkat (-ti), worth, merit
mal, property; *-e mal olmak*, to cost
memnūn, glad, pleased
otomatik, automatic
sıra, right moment, turn
-e sokmak, to insert in, push into
sual (-li), question
tasarı, bill, draft law
ucuz, cheap
yanmak, to be burned (colloquially ' to be done for, have had it ')
yılan, snake

Exercise 14

Translate into English : (1) Kavga eder-cesine konuşmıyalım. (2) Meğer koynumuzda yılan besliyormuşuz. (3) Ankaradan ayrılırken üzülüyorum; nitekim İstanbuldan ayrılışım da bana hüzün vermişti. (4) Beni yemeğe beklemişsiniz; halbuki (oysa ki) benim bu davetten haberim yoktu. (5) Ya ablanız . . . o gelmiyecek mi? (6) Aşkolsun hocam sizden bunu hiç beklemezdim! —Hayrola oğlum ne oldu? (7) Hele siz öyle söylememeli idiniz. (8) O da bu işlere burnunu soktu ha? (9) Sakın söylediklerimi unutmayın. (10) Bir görürse yandık. (11) Âdeta koğulmuştu, artık gelmez diyorduk, işte yine geldi. (12) Herkes gitti, bir o kaldı. (13) Gözü çıkasıca! (14) Bu da fazla sual ya! (15) Çocukların elbisesi bolca biçilmelidir. (16) Hallerinde benim gelişimden memnun olmadıklarını gösteren bir kekremsilik vardı. (17) Bir şeyin ucuz veya pahalı olması her vakit mal olduğu fiyata (fiate) bağlı değildir. (18) Sırası gelen memur otomatik olarak terfi ederdi. Öğrendiğimize göre yeni tasarıda memurlar zamana değil liyakate göre terfi edecekler, hattâ icabında bir senede üç defa bile terfi eyli-yebil-eceklerdir.

LESSON FIFTEEN

172. MODES OF ADDRESS

From the beginning of 1935, every Turkish family was obliged by law to choose a surname; the old titles *Bey* (' Sir '), *Paşa* (' Lord '), *Efendi* (' Master ') and *Hanım* (' Lady '), all following the name, were replaced by *Bay* (' Mr.') and *Bayan* (' Mrs., Miss '), abbreviated *B.* and *Bn.* respectively. The new terms have not yet fully caught on, being little used except on envelopes, for official purposes and by tram-conductors and other minor public servants. For social purposes, *Bay Hasan Yürükoğlu* and *Bayan Şelâle Öztürk* will be generally known as *Hasan Bey* and *Şelâle Hanım*. *Beyefendi* and *Hanımefendi* are even politer alternatives. Note *Müdür Bey*, ' Monsieur le Directeur '.

Efendi, formerly a title of royal princes, religious dignitaries and other literates, is still sometimes applied, e.g., to elderly manservants: *İbrahim Efendi*. It also means ' gentleman ', just as *hanım* means ' lady '. *Efendim* is used: (*a*) to ask for repetition of something not clearly heard—' Pardon? '—even when addressing women or children; (*b*) to give one time to think between words: *Her türlü meyva var, elma, armut, incir . . . efendim . . . portakal*, ' There's every sort of fruit; apples, pears, figs . . . er . . . oranges '.

' My friend ' is *kardeşim* (' my brother/sister '). ' My dear fellow ' is *can-ım* (' my soul ') or *azizim*. Still more affectionate is *iki gözüm* (' my two eyes ').

Although the harem is a thing of the past, there is still a trace of it in the number of alternatives for *karı*, ' wife ': *refika, zevce, âile* (' family '), *hanım* (*İsmail'in hanımı*, ' Ismail's lady '), *eş* (' mate ', also = ' husband '). A polite formula for asking after the health of the wife of a man of one's own age is: *Yenge hanım nasıl?* (' How is the lady my-brother's-wife? ').

Distinguish *very* carefully between *karıkoca* (' wife-husband '), ' a married couple ' and *kocakarı*, ' old woman, old hag '.

173. THE ARABIC AND PERSIAN ELEMENT IN TURKISH

As has been mentioned in the Introduction, the fact that there are a great many Arabic and Persian borrowings in Turkish need not worry the student, who when speaking his mother-tongue probably has no difficulty in using words like ' recognition ', ' geography ' and even ' vice versa ' and ' hoi polloi ', without necessarily being a Classical scholar. He may find it instructive, though not essential, to observe how most Arabic words are based on three-letter roots fitted to various vowel-patterns. Words containing the letters *k-t-b*, for example, all have some connection with the concept of writing:

> *kitab-*, book
> *mekteb-*, school
> *mektub-*, letter
> *kâtib-*, secretary

(1) The chief borrowing from Persian syntax was the *i* which in Persian is used to link two nouns or noun and adjective, as in ' Koh-i-Noor ', ' Mountain-of-Light '. Although this method of joining words is the exact reverse of the Turkish method, it was extensively used in the official and literary language. One of the greatest achievements of the Language Reform has been to bring about the disappearance of this affectation except in a few set expressions. ' Disappointment ', now *hayal sukut-u* (' imagining its-collapse '; two Arabic words joined according to the laws of Turkish grammar) was formerly *sukut-u hayal* (' collapse-of imagining '; the same words joined as they would be in Persian).

One use of the Persian construction which seems assured of survival in Turkish is seen in the word for ' same ', *aynı*, which is in origin the Arabic *'ayn* meaning ' very self, counterpart ' and the Persian *-i* meaning ' of ': *aynı adam*, ' the same man ', originally meant ' the-very-self-of the man '. *aynı yoldan geldik*, ' we came by the same road '. But to translate ' the same *as* ', the Turkish 3rd-person possessive suffix is used: *Bu gömlek sizinki-nin ayn-ı-dır*, ' This shirt is the same as yours ' (' of-yours its-counterpart '). The possessive suffix is often doubled in this use: *Kumaşın aynısı kalmamış*, ' There's none of the same cloth left '.

(2) A much-used Persian suffix is *-hâne*, ' house ', usually contracted to *-ne* after *a*:

> *kütüp-hane*, library (*kütüp*, Arabic plural of *kitap*, book)
> *postâne*, post-office (*posta-hane*)
> *hastâne*, hospital (*hasta-hane*)
> *eczâne*, druggist's, chemist's shop (*eczâ-hâne*, see (3) below)

(3) Some Arabic plurals are still in use (cf. our 'data, formulæ, cherubim'): *müşkül*, 'difficult', *müşkülât*, 'difficulties'; *zât*, 'person', plural *zevât* as well as *zatlar*. *Eşyâ*, the Arabic plural of *şey*, 'thing', has a different sense from *şeyler*; it means 'furniture, belongings' (cf. 'I packed my *things*'). *Eczâ*, plural of *cüz*, 'part', means 'drugs, chemicals' or 'the unbound parts of a book'. Note the pseudo-Arabic plural *gidişat*, 'goings-on', from *gidiş*, 'manner-of-going'.

(4) Several Arabic plurals are used as singulars in Turkish: *amele*, 'workman', *talebe*, 'student', *tüccar*, 'merchant', are all originally plurals. The singular of the last is also used: *tâcir*, so 'merchants' is *tüccarlar* or *tacirler*. Cf. *eşyalar* in Exercise 15, No. 8.

(5) The Arabic verbal nouns which, with *etmek*, make compound verbs in Turkish, retain their verbal force even without *etmek*, and so can have an object in the def. obj. case:

> *tefrik etmek*, to distinguish
> *Renkler-i tefrik edebilir misiniz?* Can you distinguish the colours?
> *Renkler-i tefrik kolay-dır*, It is easy to distinguish the colours.
> *Konya'yı ziyaret ettik*, We visited Konya.
> *Konya'yı ziyaretimiz*, our visiting K., our visit to K.

(6) The Arabic preposition *ilâ*, 'to', is used between numbers: *sekiz ila on beş milyon lira*, '8-15 million liras'. This is the only preposition used independently in Turkish, as distinct from those which form part of Arabic phrases, like the *bi-* ('in') of *bilhassa*, 'in particular, especially'.

(7) In Arabic, adjectives are made from nouns by the addition of long *i*. In Turkish this long *i* is written with a circumflex accent only to avoid confusion with similar words (§ 12 (2)):

> *tarih*, history; *tarihi*, its history; *tarihî*, historical
> *ilim*, science; *ilmi*, its science; *ilmî*, scientific

But—*iktisat*, economy; *iktisadı*, its economy; *iktisadi*, economic

Note *millî*, 'national' (*millet*, 'nation'), but *milli*, 'furnished with a spike' (*mil*; cf. § 86).

An unsuccessful attempt has been made to replace this useful suffix by -*(s)el*, with hardly any more justification than the existence of an adjective *uysal*, 'compliant, easy-going'; cf. *uymak*,

' to conform '.   One sometimes comes across *tarihsel*, ' historical ', for *tarihî*; *siyasal*, ' political ', for *siyasi*; *ulusal*, ' national ', (*ulus*, ' nation ') for *millî*.

174. FORMATION OF VERBS

The following are the chief suffixes used to make verbs from other parts of speech (cf. our ' -ize, -ify ') :

(1) *-lemek*

  göz, eye; *gözlemek*, to keep an eye on, watch out for
  su, water; *sulamak*, to water, irrigate
  tekrar, again; *tekrarlamak*, to repeat
  hazır, ready; *hazırlamak*, to prepare

(2) *-lenmek* (the preceding plus the reflexive *n*—§ 137)

  hazırlanmak, to prepare oneself
  ev, house, home; *evlenmek*, to get married
  can, life, soul; *canlanmak*, to come to life

(3) *-leşmek* (*-lemek* plus *ş*—§ 150)

  avrupa-lı, European; *avrupalılaşmak*, to be Europeanized
  dert, pain; *dertleşmek*, to commiserate with one another
  mektup, letter; *mektuplaşmak*, to exchange letters, correspond
  bir, one; *birleşmek*, to become one, unite
  ölmez, not-dying; *ölmezleşmek*, to become immortal

(4) *-(e)lmek*

  doğru-lmak, *kısa-lmak*, *yüce-lmek*, to become straight, short, high
  az-almak, *düz-elmek*, *çoğ-almak*, to become small, orderly, numerous

Two-syllabled words ending in a *k* lose it before this suffix :

  küçük, small; *küçü-lmek*, to become small
  yüksek, high; *yükse-lmek*, to become high, to rise

(5) *-ermek*

With words of more than one syllable, only the first syllable is used before this suffix, which is added mostly to names of colours :

  ak, white; *ağ-armak*, to turn white
  sarı, yellow; *sar-armak*, to turn yellow
  yeşil, green; *yeş-ermek*, to turn green
  kızıl, red; *kız-armak*, to turn red, to blush, to be roasted or fried

(6) -(im)semek

>   su, water; susamak, to be thirsty
>   mühim, important; mühimsemek, to consider important
>   benim, of me; benimsemek, to appropriate
>   çok, much; çoğumsamak, to regard as excessive
>   az, little; azımsamak, to consider insufficient

Note : Causatives are formed regularly: sula-t-mak, ' to cause
to irrigate '; canlan-dır-mak, ' to revive, vivify '; ölmezleş-tir-mek,
' to immortalize '; düzel-t-mek, ' to level, put in order '; kızar-t-
mak, ' to roast, fry '.

175. FORMATION OF NOUNS AND ADJECTIVES

The following list of suffixes does not aim at completeness but
will often help the student to guess at the meaning of a noun or
adjective from a knowledge of a kindred verb. To save space
the infinitive ending -mek has been omitted.

(1) -gi

>   çiz-, to draw; çizgi, line
>   ser-, to spread out; sergi, display, fair
>   duy-, to feel; duygu, feeling, sensation
>   iç-, to drink; içki (§ 44), alcoholic drink

(2) -gen

>   atıl-, to be thrown, hurl oneself; atılgan, reckless
>   çekin-, to withdraw; çekingen, shy
>   unut-, to forget; unutkan, forgetful
>   çalış-, to work; çalışkan, hard-working

(3) -gin

>   gir-, to enter; girgin, pushful
>   kes-, to cut; keskin, sharp
>   uy-, to conform; uygun, suitable
>   kaç-, to flee; kaçkın, fugitive

(4) -i

>   ölç-, to measure; ölçü, measure, dimension
>   öl-, to die; ölü, corpse
>   yap-, to make; yapı, construction
>   yaz-, to write; yazı, writing, article

Note : kazı ' diggings ', coined from kaz- ' to dig ', to replace the
Arabic hafriyat ' excavations '.

(5) -(i)k

    kes-, to cut; *kesik*, cut, broken

    aç-, to open; *açık*, open(ed)

    boz-, to destroy; *bozuk*, destroyed, corrupt

    parla-, to shine; *parlak*, bright

    karış-, to become confused; *karışık*, disordered

    Note : Birleşik Amerika Devletleri, ' U.S.A. ' (§ 174 (3)).

(6) -im

    öl-, to die; *ölüm*, death

    doğ-, to be born; *doğum*, birth (*doğumevi*, maternity home)

    kaldır-, to raise; *kaldırım*, pavement

    iç-, to drink; *içim*, (one) drink (*bir içim su*, a drink of water)

(7) -inti

    süpür-, to sweep; *süprüntü*, sweepings

    ak-, to flow; *akıntı*, current

    sars-, to shake; *sarsıntı*, tremor

(8) -ç

    sevin-, to be pleased; *sevinç*, joy

    kazan, to win; *kazanç*, gain, profit

    iğren-, to feel loathing; *iğrenç*, loathsome

176. Notes on Certain Verbs

(1) *bulunmak*, ' to be found, to be ': *Ankara'da bulunan bir arkadaşım*, ' A friend of mine *who is* in A.', but *Ankara'da olan bir vaka*, ' an event *which occurs* in A.'

The construction of § 130 (*b*) is applied to other nouns beside the *-mek* infinitive, with *bulunmak* for the verb ' to be ':

    Onunla çok münākaşa-da bulunduk, We had an intense dispute with him (we-found-ourselves in much dispute with him)

    göndermek nezaket-inde bulduğunuz kitap, the book which you were kind enough to send (pertaining-to-your-being in-the-kindness of to-send)

(2) *buyurmak*, ' to order ', is used as a courteous substitute for other verbs:

    Buyurun ! Do please come in/help yourself/sit down.

    Bize buyurmaz mısınız ? Won't you deign to call on us?

    Ne buyurdunuz ? What did you say?

(3) *durmak*, ' to stand ', means ' to continue, keep on ': (*a*)
When suffixed to the *-e* adverbial form of another verb: *yaza-
durmak*, ' to keep on writing '. (*b*) More frequently it follows the
-ıp form: *yazıp durmak*. (*c*) It sometimes follows in the same
tense as the first verb: *Bütün gün yazdı durdu*, ' The whole day he
kept on writing '.

durup dururken (' while standing and standing ') means ' suddenly and without warning '.

şöyle dursun (' let-it-stand thus ') means ' let alone ': *Cevap
vermek şöyle dursun*; *mektubunu okumadım bile*, ' I haven't even read
his letter, let alone answer (it) '.

(4) *etmek* and *yapmak*. The usual equivalent of ' to make, do ',
is *yapmak*:

> *O size hiç bir şey yapamaz*, He can't do a thing to you.
> *Orada ne yapıyorsunuz ?* What are you doing there?
> *Bu makina çok gürültü yapıyor*, This engine is making a lot of
>   noise.

If a normally transitive compound verb is used without an
object, *etmek* is replaced by *yapmak*: *Masraf-ım-ı hesab-ediyorum*, ' I
am calculating my expenses ', but *Hesap yapıyorum*, ' I am calculating '. So, too, if the verbal-noun part of the compound is
qualified: *bana tesir etti*, ' it influenced me ', but *bana yaptığı
tesir*, ' the influence which it had on me '.

Etmek translates ' to make ' in, e.g., ' 10 + 10 make 20 '—*on,
on daha yirmi eder*—and ' to do ' with words meaning ' good ' or
' bad ': *Bunu yapmak-la fena mı ettim ?* ' Did I do wrong by-doing
this ? '

(5) *gelmek*, ' to come ', used after the *-e* adverbial form of
another verb denotes continuous action:

> *Bu işler böyle olagelmiş*, These affairs have gone on (' con-
>   tinued-to-be ') thus.
> *yapagelmek*, to continue to do

The sole exception is *çıkagelmek*, which means ' to come up suddenly ', *not* ' to keep coming up '.

With the ablative, less commonly the dative, of the negative
infinitive in *-memezlik* (§ 129 (2)) it gives the sense of ' to pretend
not to ': *işitmemezlikten geldim* or *işitmemezliğe geldim*, ' I pretended
not to hear '.

Uyku-m geldi (my sleep has come), I feel sleepy.

. . . *göreceğim geldi* (my-future-seeing . . . has come), I feel I must see . . .

Öyle gibi-m-e geliyor ki, It seems to me that . . .

Lâzım geliyor, it is necessary.

(6) *gitmek*, ' to go ': there is a common idiom with this word and the adjectives *hoş, tuhaf, güç*, ' pleasant, curious, difficult ':

Hoş-unuz-a gidiyor mu? (Does it go to-your-pleasant?) Do you like it?

Pek hoş-um-a gitmiyor, I don't like it much.

Tuhaf-ım-a gitti, It struck me as odd.

Güc-üm-e gitti, It offended me.

(7) *kalmak*, ' to remain, be left ', is used after the *-e* adverbial form of other verbs:

şaş-tı, he was surprised; *şaşakaldı* (he-was-left being-surprised), he was dumbfounded

donmak, to freeze; *donakalmak*, to be left freezing, to be petrified

Note also:

Nerede kaldınız? Where have you been?

Bana kalırsa, If it is left to me, if you ask me.

Az kaldı (little remained), almost; *Az kaldı ağlamağa başlıyacaktım*, I was within an ace of starting to cry.

Kaldı ki . . . There remained the fact that . . ., Furthermore . . .

(8) *olmak*, ' to become ', is used with nouns, particularly names of diseases, to mean ' to fall victim to, catch ':

Tifo oldu, He's got typhoid.

Öksürük oldu, He's caught a cough.

defolmak (to become repulsion), to clear off; *Defol!* Hop it!

Cehennem ol! Go to hell!

Note also:

Olan oldu, It's happened now; there's nothing we can do.

Oldu olacak, The worst has happened; *Oldu olacak bari ben de geleyim*, Oh, well, in that case I may as well come too.

F

(9) *-e uğramak*, ' to drop in on, touch at, meet with '. often of something unpleasant:

> *felâket-e uğramak*, to meet with disaster
> *hayal sukutu-na uğramak*, to be disappointed (§ 173 (1))
> *tehir-e uğramak*, to be postponed

The causative *uğratmak* is ' to expose to ': *Beni hayal sukutuna uğrattınız*, ' You have disappointed me '.

(10) *vermek*, ' to give ', when joined to another verb-stem by *-(y)i-*, adds the notion of speed:

> *Gel-i-ver!* Come quickly!
> *Otobüs dur-u-verdi*, The bus stopped suddenly.
> *yaz-ı-vermek*, to scribble, to dash off

(11) *yemek*, ' to eat ', is used of undergoing something, usually unpleasant:

> *tokat yemek*, to get a box on the ear
> *yağmur yemek*, to get caught in the rain
> *gol yemek*, to have a goal scored against one

But—

> *mirās yemek*, to receive a legacy
> *rüşvet yemek*, to take bribes

177. GREETINGS AND POLITE EXPRESSIONS

Merhaba! ' Hallo! ' (should not be used to older people or ladies).

Günaydın, ' Good morning '.

Hoş geldiniz, ' Welcome '—answer *Hoş bulduk*.

Ne var ne yok? ' What's doing, how are things? '—answer *İyilik sağlık*.

Geceler hayrolsun or *Allah rahatlık versin*, ' Good night '.

Allaha ısmarladık (often pronounced *Allasmarladık*, ' We have committed to God ') or *Hoşça kalın*, ' Good-bye ', said by person leaving—answer *Güle güle*, ' (Go) laughingly '.

On being introduced: *Müşerref oldum*, ' I have become honoured '—answer *Şeref bana ait*, ' The honour (is) belonging to me '.

İnşallāh (Arabic), ' if God wishes ', used when making any plans, even for the immediate future: *Bu akşam gidiyor musunuz yani?*—*İnşallah*, ' That means you're going this evening? '—Please God! '

Maşallāh (Arabic), 'whatever God wishes', expresses admiration while at the same time warding off the evil eye. It should always be used when admiring children.

When seeing someone about to eat: *Āfiyet olsun*, 'let there be health, *bon appétit*'—answer *Ömrünüz çok olsun*, 'May your life be long', or simply *Teşekkür ederim*.

When refusing an invitation to a meal: *Ziyāde olsun*, 'May there be superabundance'.

When a friend pays the bill or buys the tickets: *Kesenize bereket*, 'Blessing to your purse'.

(*Sizde*) *kalsın* ('let it remain with you'), 'Keep the change'.

When your host offers you coffee he will probably ask: *Nasıl içersiniz?* 'How do you drink (it)?' The alternatives are: *sāde*, 'plain' = *şekersiz*, 'sugarless'; *az, orta* or *çok şekerli*, 'little-, medium-, much-sugared'.

When taking leave of your host: *Bendenize müsāade*, 'Permission for-your-servant', or *Bana müsāade*.

Baş üstüne, 'On the head', i.e., 'On my head be it. It shall be done'.

178. DOUBLETS

(1) We have met numerous instances of the doubling of words to denote intensity, e.g., §§ 96 (2), 99 (2), 112. Turkish is very fond also of using similar-sounding pairs of words, like our 'kith and kin', 'moiling and toiling'. Cf. § 154 (3). Note also:

> *çoluk çocuk*, wife and family
> *boy bos*, size and shape (of persons)
> *iş güç* (work-toil), employment
> *yatak yorgan* (bed-quilt), bed and bedding
> *yorgun argın* (tired-emaciated), dead beat
> *ufak tefek*, small and trifling, odds and ends
> *alaca bulaca*, all the colours of the rainbow

Çoluk, bos, tefek are not used except in these expressions.

(2) Words which imitate sounds are usually doubled:

> *şap şap öpmek*, to kiss with a smacking sound
> *horul horul horlamak*, to snore like a pig
> *tık tık etmek*, to tick, tap

(3) A common colloquial way of emphasizing an adjective is seen in *Babası zengin mi zengin*, 'Is her father rich? Rich!'—rather like the American 'Is he rich or is he rich?'

Vocabulary 15

binā, building
bulut (*-tu*), cloud
cilt, binding of a book, volume;
　ciltli, bound
çatal, fork, forked, ambiguous
çeşit, kind, sort
dede, grandfather
eksik, deficiency, deficient,
　wanting
hummā, fever
idāre, administration
istifāde, benefit, advantage
kapı, gate, door
kat (*-tı*), fold, storey
konsolos, consul
koyun (*-ynu*), bosom
koyun (*-yunu*), sheep
kurtulmak, to be saved, escape
lezzet (*-ti*), pleasure, enjoyment
mâkul (*-lü*), reasonable
-e mecbur, obliged to
mevsūk (*-ku*), trustworthy, re-
　liable

miktar, quantity
mukāyese etmek, to compare
mühendis, engineer
mürācaat (*-tı*), recourse, applica-
　tion
nakletmek, to remove, transfer
nevi (*-v'i*), species
öğretim, teaching, schooling
peş, the space behind anything;
　peşinden koşmak, to run after it
　(§ 126)
silâh, weapon, arm
Sofya, Sofia (capital of *Bul-
　garistan*, Bulgaria)
spor, sport, games
şahsan, personally
tamam, complete, perfect
tatmak (*tad-*), to taste
telgraf çekmek, to send a tele-
　gram, to wire
yavru, the young of an ani-
　mal
zarf, envelope

Exercise 15

Translate into English : (1) Hangi silâhlarla silâh-lan-ır-sa
silâhlan-sın, ölümden kurtulamıyacak. (2) Eyvah! İşler çatal-
laştı. (3) Kapı kapı dolaşıp onu aradık. (4) Dün gece dede-
m-in koyunlarından biri yavru-la-mış. (5) Mektubu zarfa
koymak üzere iki-ye kat-la-dı. (6) Hava bulut-lan-ıyor. Galiba
yağmur yağacak. (7) Bir kişi eksik-ti, şimdi tamam-lan-dık.
(8) Eşyalarımı yollamaları için oraya telgraf çekmek istiyorum.
(9) İş-i güc-ü olmayıp şurada burada dolaşan kimselere ' Kaldırım
mühendisi ' derler. (10) Bu kitabın ecza-sı ciltlisinden elli kuruş
eksiğine sat-ıl-ır. (11) Yazma ve basma her çeşit eski kitaplar
satın alınır. Çok miktarda kitaplar, adam gönder-il-erek yerinde
alınır. Şahsan veya mektupla idare-hane-mize müracaat. (12)
Bina-nın spor ve kütüphane salonları eski-si gibi gençliğin isti-
fadesine açık bulun-dur-ul-acak-tır. (13) Dedem gazetesini

oku-r-ken uyu-yu-vermiş. (14) Siz bu iki şey-i mukayese ediyor-
sunuz ama, bu yaptığınız mukayese yerinde değil. Çünkü
mukayese-si-ni yaptığınız şeyler aynı nevi-den değildir. (15)
Her yıl eylûl son-una kadar altı yaşını bit-ir-miş olanlar on dört
yaşını tamam-la-dık-ları öğretim yılı sonuna kadar ilk okul-a
devam-a mecbur-dur-lar. (16) Olmıyacak bir işin peşinden
koş-maktansa, hayatın lezzetini, el-e geç-tiğ-i yerde hemen tad-ı-
vermek şüphesiz ki daha mâkul-dür. (17) Mevsuk kaynaklardan
bil-dir-il-diğ-i-ne göre, Varna Konsolosluğu Sofya Konsolosluğuna
nakledilerek iki konsolosluk birleştirilmiştir. (18) Sık sık hasta-
lanır, humma başlar başlamaz İstanbul sularını sayıkla-r-dı
(§ 102, *Note*).

LESSON SIXTEEN

179. How to Read Turkish

The large number of adverbial forms of the verb makes it easy for the Turkish writer to ramble happily on, with an *-ip*, an *-erek* or an *-ince* linking one thought to the next, for line after line. Although most modern writers prefer to keep their sentences short, a practice now taught in Turkish schools, one must be prepared for reversions to type.

Here is a sentence from *Beş Şehir*, a recent work by Ahmet Hamdi Tanpınar: ' Topkapıdaki Ahmediye camiinin caddeye yakın kapısından veya bu caddenin herhangi bir boş arsasından, bir yığın yangın yerinin üstünden atlıyarak gördüğümüz âbideler şehriyle, Yedikule kahvelerinden baktığımız zaman deniz kenarındaki sur parçalariyle büyük camileri birbirine âdeta ekliyen mehtaplı manzara arasında ne kadar fark vardır.'

The first step is to glance over the sentence to get the general pattern and then to look at the end for the verb: *vardır*, ' there is '. Now begin working back to find *what* there is: *ne kadar fark*, ' how much difference '; *arasında*, ' between '. In § 126 (5) we saw that nouns followed by this word are linked by *ile*; and there in the middle is *şehriyle*, ' the city of . . . and ', the word before *arasında*: *manzara*, ' scene '. Now we have the skeleton of the sentence; the difference between the city of something and the something scene. ' City of ' *âbideler*, ' monuments '; *gördüğümüz*, ' which we see '; *Topkapıdaki A. camiinin . . . kapısından*, ' from the gate of the Ahmediye mosque at Topkapı '. Then a phrase preceding and qualifying *kapı-*: *caddeye yakın*, ' near to the main road '; *veya bu caddenin*, ' or of this road '; *herhangi bir boş arsasından*, ' from any vacant building-plot of it '; *üstünden atlıyarak (atlamak*: § 88, *Note*), ' by-jumping over-the-top '; *bir yığın yangın yerinin*, ' of a heap of (§ 140) conflagration-place '; *(şehri)-yle*, ' and '; *mehtaplı manzara*, ' the moonlit scene '; *âdeta ekliyen (eklemek)*, ' virtually linking '; *büyük camileri*, ' the great mosques '; *birbirine*, ' to one another '; *sur parçalariyle*, ' with the portions of city-wall '; *deniz kenarındaki*, ' which are on the sea-shore'; *baktığımız zaman*, 'the time pertaining-to-our-looking'; *Yedikule kahvelerinden*, 'from the cafés of Yedikule'.

Putting it all together, and with only the changes necessary to make intelligible English: 'What a difference there is between the city of monuments, which we can see from the gate, nearest to the main road, of the Ahmediye Mosque at Topkapı, or, by jumping over a heap of burnt rubble, from any vacant site along this road, and the moonlit scene which appears to link the great mosques one to another with the portions of the city-wall along the sea-shore, when we look out from the coffee-houses of Yedikule'.

An English author would probably make three sentences of it: 'On the one hand the city of. . . . On the other hand the moonlit scene. . . . What a contrast between the two!'

180. FOR FURTHER READING

An admirable selection of annotated passages will be found in P. Wittek's *Turkish Reader* (Lund Humphries), which has a vocabulary of almost 4000 words. When that has been worked through, the student should be able to cope with any modern Turkish work, with the help of a dictionary. The *Oxford Turkish Dictionary*, by Fahir İz and H. C. Hony, is in two volumes, Turkish–English and English–Turkish, and is particularly rich in the idiomatic expressions which are a part of the fascination of Turkish.

Advanced students will learn much from *Türkçe Sözlük*, the Turkish–Turkish dictionary published by the Turkish Language Society (Türk Dil Kurumu) of Ankara. This work gives numerous examples showing the use of words in sentences, and contains all the neologisms one is likely to meet, even in books written at the height of the Language Reform Movement.

181. POETIC AND CONVERSATIONAL WORD-ORDER

In poetry the rules of normal word-order may be relaxed to meet the demands of metre and rhyme; a sentence such as *Yaz-ın son yemiş-ler-i-ne daha doy-ma-mış-tık*, 'We had not yet had our fill of the last fruits of summer', may become in poetry *Daha doymamıştık son yemişlerine yazın*.

In conversation too, Turks, like other people, often depart from the strict rules of literary word-order. One tends to say first the word that is uppermost in one's mind. *Yangın var! Kaçın*

sağdaki kapıdan, ' Fire! Get out through the door on the right! '
Kaçın is the important word, and cannot wait to take its proper
place at the end of the sentence. *Sahib-i var oranın*, ' It's taken,
that place' (' its-possessor exists, of-that-place '). *Gitti mi
arkadaşınız?* ' Has he gone, your friend? '

There is a school of writers who use this essentially conversational freedom even in passages which do not reproduce conversation. The beginner will be well advised to adhere to the literary
order of words, in speaking and writing, until he has attained some
familiarity with the language.

182. SLANG

The last sentence of the preceding paragraph applies also to
one's choice of vocabulary. Turks are so unaccustomed to
Englishmen who can speak any Turkish at all, that the visitor
to Turkey will find plenty of help and encouragement when he
tries to make himself understood in Turkish. But few things
sound sillier than out-of-date slang, or slang used in the wrong
place. So if slang is to be learned at all it must be learned on
the spot and not from books. Anyone who has heard a visitor
from the Continent say to his hostess, " It was a topping party,
but now I must sling my hook ", will see the force of these remarks.

183. SUMMARY OF VERBAL FORMS

The table below shows the various combinations of the bases,
given in the first column, with the personal endings, indicated
by Roman figures (§ 66), and with those parts of the verb ' to be '
which are based on the stem *i*-, namely *idi*, ' he was ' (§ 82); *ise*,
' if he is ' (§ 158); and *imiş*, ' he is/was said to be ' (§ 134).

A slanting line shows that the combination belonging in that
position in the table does not exist; e.g., the dubitative *imiş*
cannot be attached to the definite *geldi*. Bracketed forms are
not much used.

The Type III endings occur only with the Imperative (not
shown here; see § 128), the Type IV endings only with the
Subjunctive.

To simplify the table, the combinations of *imiş* with *idim* have
not been included, e.g., *geliyormuştum*, ' they say/said that I was
coming '; *gelmiş imiştim*, ' they say/said that I had come '.

	idi (II)	*ise* (II)	*imiş* (I)
			THEY SAY/SAID THAT:
geliyor (§ 88) geliyorum (I) I am coming	geliyordum I was coming	geliyorsam If I am coming	geliyormuşum I am coming
gelir (§ 105) gelirim (I) I come	gelirdim I used to come	gelirsem If I come	gelirmişim I come
gelecek (§ 102) geleceğim (I) I shall come	gelecektim I should come	geleceksem If I am about to come	gelecekmişim I shall come
gelmeli (§ 153) gelmeliyim (I) I ought to come	gelmeliydim I ought to have come	gelmeliysem If I ought to come	gelmeliymişim I ought to come
gelmiş (§ 135) gelmişim (I) I have come	gelmiştim I had come	gelmişsem If I have come	gelmiş imişim I have come
geldi (§ 81) geldim (II) I came, have come	geldiydim I had come	geldiysem If I came	
gelse (§ 158) gelsem (II) If I were to come	gelseydim If only I came		(gelseymişim) If I were to come
gele (§ 159) geleyim (IV) (that) I may come	geleydim (that) I might come		(geleymişim) I may come

APPENDIX

Glossary of Military Terms

Note : in the Turkish words given below, the 3rd-person possessive suffix has been hyphenated, to show that, e.g., ' at the air base ' is *hava üssünde* (§ 71).

Air base, *hava üss-ü*
Aircraft carrier, *uçak gemi-si*
Airfield, aerodrome, *hava meydan-ı*
    ,,   construction battalion, *hava meydanı inşa tabur-u*
Air force, *hava kuvvet-i*
    Royal Air Force, *Krallık Hava Kuvvetler-i*
Air raid, *hava akın-ı*
Ally, *müttefik (-ki)*
Ammunition, *cephane*
    ,,   -dump, *cephane depo-su*
Anti-aircraft battery, *uçaksavar batarya*
    ,,   gun, *uçaksavar top*
Anti-tank rifle, *tank savar tüfek*
Arm-chair General, *salon general-i*
Armistice, *mütāreke*
Armour(ed), *zırh(lı)*
Army, *ordu*
Artillery(-man), *topçu*
    ,,   barrage, *topçu baraj-ı*
Attack, *taarruz*
  to attack, *-e taarruz etmek*
Barracks, *kışla*
Base, *üs (-ssü)*
    ,,   Camp, *üs kamp-ı*
Battle, *muhārebe*
Bayonet, *süngü*
Bazooker, *bazuka*
Bomb, *bomba*
    ,,   Anti-personnel, *personele karşı bomba*
    ,,   Atom, *atom bomba-sı*
    ,,   H.E., *yüksek infilâklı bomba*

Bomb, Hydrogen, *hidrojen bomba-sı*
  ,,   Incendiary, *yangın bomba-sı*
  ,,   Napalm, *jelâtinli benzin bomba-sı*
  ,,   Smoke, *sis bomba-sı*
  to bomb, *bombalamak, bombardıman etmek*
Bomber, *bombardıman uçağ-ı*
Bombproof, *bomba geçmez*
Bulldozer, *arāzi düzeltme makine-si, buldozer*
Bullet, *kurşun*
Camouflage, *gizleme, kamuflâj*
Casualties, *zāyıat (-tı)*
  to suffer casualties, *zayıat vermek*
  dead (Turkish), *şehit* (' Martyr for the Faith ')
  dead (other nationalities), *ölü*
  wounded, *yaralı*
  missing, *(harpte) kayıp*
  prisoner, *esir*
Cavalry, *süvari*
Commander, *komutan*
Commando *akıncı bölüğ-ü, komando*
Conscript soldier, *kur'a er-i*
Convalescent Depot, *nekāhet merkez-i*
Counter-espionage, *casusluğa karşı korunma*
Defeat, *mağlûbiyet*
  to defeat, *mağlûp etmek, yenmek*
Defence, *müdāfaa*
  to defend, *müdafaa etmek*
Deserter, *asker kaçağ-ı*
to dig in, *siper kazıp mevzilenmek, siper kazıp mevzi almak* (' to dig
    trenches and take position ')
to disembark, *karaya çık(ar)mak* (§ 151 (6))
to embark, *gemiye bin(dir)mek*
Embarkation leave, *bindirme izn-i*
Enemy, *düşman*
to enlist, join up, *asker yazılmak*
to fight with, *-le çarpışmak*
Fighter, *avcı uçağ-ı*
    ,,   escort, *muhāfız (himāye) av uçaklar-ı*
Flame-thrower, *alev cihaz-ı*
Fortifications, *tahkimat (-tı)*
  to fortify, *tahkim etmek*
Front, *cephe*

Front line, *cephe hatt-ı*

Gas, *gaz*

„ mask, *gaz maske-si*

Ground forces, *kara kuvvetler-i*

Halt! Who goes there? *Dur! Kim o?*

—Friend, —*Yabancı değil!*

Hand grenade, *el bomba-sı*

Headquarters, *karargâh*

Helicopter, *helikopter*

Hospital ship, *hasta nakliye gemi-si*

Infantry, *piyade*

Insecticide, *haşerat öldürücü ilâç*

Intelligence, *istihbārāt*

„ Officer, *istihbārāt subay-ı*

Interpreter, *tercüman*

Jet aircraft, *tepkili uçak*

Leave, *izin(-zni)*

on leave, *izinli*

Liaison Officer, *irtibat subay-ı*

Lorry, *kamyon*

Machine gun, *makineli tüfek*

Manœuvres, *manevra(lar)*

Medical Officer, *askerî doktor*

„ Orderly, *sıhhiye er-i*

Military (adjective), *askerî*

„ Policeman, *askerî inzibat erbaş-ı*

Mine, *mayn, mayın*

„ -field, *mayn tarla-sı*

„ -layer, *mayn salan gemi*

„ -sweeper, *mayn tarayıcı gemi, arama tarama gemi-si*

Mobilization, *seferberlik*

Mortar, *havan top-u*

Navy, *donanma*

Orderly, *emir er-i*

„ Officer, *nöbetçi subay-ı*

Parachutist, *paraşütçü*

Password, *parola*

Prisoner of war, *harp esir-i*

„ „ camp, *esir kamp-ı*

Radar, *radar*

Radio navigational aids, *uçuşa yardım radyo tesisat-ı*

Red Crescent, *Kızılay*

Red Cross, *Kızıl Haç* (-*çı*)
Regular Army, *muvazzaf ordu*
Reinforcements, replacements, *takviye birlikler-i*
Rifle, *tüfek*
Rocket, *füze*
Sailor, *gemici*
Self-propelled gun, *zatülhareke top*
Sentry, *nöbetçi*
 to post sentries, *nöbetçi dikmek*
Shell, *mermi*
Shrapnel, *şarapnel*
Signal Corps, *muhābere sınıf-ı*
Soldier, *asker*
Spy, *cāsus*
Squadron (Air Force), *uçak bölüğ-ü*
 ,, (Naval), *gemi filo-su*
Stretcher-bearer, *sedyeci, teskereci*
Submarine, *denizaltı*
Tank, *tank* (*kı*)
 ,, -obstacle, *tank mānia-sı*
 ,, -trap, *tank tuzağ-ı*
Tommy Atkins (Turkish equivalent), *Mehmetçik*
Transit Camp, *tranzit merkez-i*
Trench, *siper*
Unit, *birlik, kıta*
Volunteer, *gönüllü*
War, *harp* (-*bi*), *savaş*
Wing, *kanad*
 Right—of the army, *ordunun sağ kanad-ı*
 Left—of the army, *ordunun sol kanad-ı*

Army Corps, *Kolordu*
Division, *Tümen*
Brigade, *Tugay*
Regiment, *Alay*
Battalion, *Tabur*
Company, *Bölük*
Platoon, *Takım*
Section, *Manga*
Battery, *Batarya*
L.M.G. Group (Infantry), *Manganın hafif makineli kısm-ı*
Rifle Group (Infantry), *Manganın avcı kısm-ı*

TABLE OF RANKS

Navy British	Navy Turkish	Army British	Army Turkish	Air Force British	Air Force Turkish
Admiral of the Fleet	Note (i)	Field Marshal	Note (i)	Marshal of the R.A.F.	Note (i)
Admiral (Senior)	Oramiral	General	Orgeneral	Air Chief Marshal (Senior)	Orgeneral
Admiral (Junior)	Koramiral	Lieut.-General	Korgeneral	Air Chief Marshal (Junior)	Korgeneral
Vice Admiral / Rear Admiral	Tümamiral / Tugamiral	Major General / —	Tümgeneral / —	Air Marshal / Air Vice Marshal	Tümgeneral / Tuggeneral
Commodore	No equiv.	Brigadier	Tuğgeneral	Air Commodore	No equiv.
Captain (Senior) / Captain (Junior) / Commander / Lieut.-Commander	Albay / Yarbay / Binbaşı / Ön Yüzbaşı	Colonel / — / Lieut.-Colonel / Major	Albay / — / Yarbay / Binbaşı	Group Captain / — / Wing Commander / Squadron Leader	Albay / — / Yarbay / Binbaşı
Lieutenant / Sub-Lieutenant / A/Sub-Lieut.	Yüzbaşı / Üsteğmen / Teğmen	Captain / Lieutenant / 2nd Lieutenant	Yüzbaşı / Üsteğmen / Teğmen	Flight Lieutenant / Flying Officer / Pilot Officer	Yüzbaşı / Üsteğmen / Teğmen
Midshipman	Asteğmen	No equiv.	Asteğmen	A/Pilot Officer	Asteğmen
		R.S.M. / C.S.M. / C.Q.M.S. / Sgt. / Cpl. / Pte.	Kıdemli Başçavuş / Başçavuş / Üstçavuş / Çavuş / Onbaşı / Er		

Note (*i*) : There are no exact equivalents of these British ranks in the Turkish forces. The titles *Büyük Amiral* (Navy) and *Mareşal* (Army and Air Force) are awarded to officers who have held a high command with distinction.

Note (*ii*): Although the table is correct for each Service, it contains, for reasons too involved to discuss here, a discrepancy in the relative ranks of the three Turkish Services: the Army *Tuğgeneral* is shown as being one rank below the Air Force *Tuğgeneral* and the Naval *Tuğamiral*, which is not the case. Service readers are asked to accept the table, discrepancy and all, as being based on the most authoritative sources available at the time of going to press.

Note (*iii*): *Subay* is the generic term for ' Officer '.

Assubaylar are ' Junior Officers ', from *Asteğmen* to *Yüzbaşı* inclusive. *Binbaşı* to *Albay* inclusive are *Üstsubaylar*, those above being collectively known as *Generaller* or *Amiraller*.

' Reserve Officer ' is *Yedek Subay*.

' N.C.O.' is *Erbaş*; Regular N.C.O.s are called *Astsubay*, formerly *Gedikli*. There are no regular private soldiers.

Note (*iv*): Graduates of the Staff College are known as Staff Officers, *Kurmay Subaylar*, whether or not they are serving on the Staff; e.g., a Colonel who is a graduate of the Staff College and is commanding an infantry regiment is referred to as *Kurmay Albay*. ' General Staff ' is *Genelkurmay*.

Note (*v*): To distinguish between Turkish officers of the Navy, Army and Air Force, the words *Deniz*, *Kara* and *Hava* respectively are put before the name of the rank, which then takes the 3rd-person possessive suffix: e.g., *Hava Yüzbaşı-sı*, ' Flight Lieutenant' (' Air its-Captain '); *Deniz Yüzbaşı-sı*, ' Naval Lieutenant '; *Kara Yüzbaşı-sı*, ' Army Captain '.

MILITARY EXTRACTS

1. Kızıllar, ağır bir topçu barajı himayesinde Türk tugayı ve 35inci Amerikan alayının tutmakta olduğu 4 kilometrelik bir cepheye taarruz etmişlerdi. Müttefik topçu ve havan topları, açtıkları baraj ateşiyle komünistleri Birleşmiş Milletler hatlarının takriben 80 metre yakınlarında durdurmuşlardır. İki saat süren şiddetli bir çarpışmayı müteakip kızıllar çekilmiştir.

kızıl, red	*takriben*, approximately
ağır, heavy	*şiddet*, violence
himāye, protection	*müteākip* (with def. obj. case), subsequent to, after

2. Teyit edildiğine göre 5 Haziran perşembe günü Kore'de Birleşmiş Milletler ideali uğrunda çarpışmakta olan Türk Tugayının cephe hattındaki tahkimatı teftiş eden Alay Komutanı Albay Nuri Pamir açılan düşman topçu ateşi neticesinde bir şarapnelin kafatasına isabeti neticesinde şehid olmuştur.

tēyit etmek, to confirm	*netice*, result
ideal (-li), ideal	*kafa-tas-ı*, skull (head its-bowl)
teftiş etmek, to inspect	*-e isābet (-ti)*, hit on

3. Geçen yıla kadar atom bombalarının ancak stratejik sahada kullanılabilecekleri, taktik alanda kullanılmaları, yalnız düşman için değil, kendi kıtaları için de tehlikeli olacağı ileri sürülmekte idi. Şimdi ise: Piyadenin de kullanabileceği taktik atom silâhlarına kadar birçok tip atom silâhları ve bombaları yapılmağa başlandığı belirtilmektedir . . . Sonra atom enerjisi ile hareket eden uçak gemileri, atom enerjisi ile hareket eden denizaltılar, atom enerjisi ile hareket eden harp uçaklarının da yapılmasına başlanmış olduğu ve bu uçak gemilerinin hiçbir yerden yakıt almadan ve bu denizaltıların hiç deniz yüzüne çıkmadan dünyayı dolaşabilecek kabiliyette olacakları belirtilmektedir.

sāha, *alan*, field, sphere of activity	*belirtmek*, to reveal, make clear
tehlike, danger	*enerji*, power, energy
ileri sürmek, to suggest (drag forward)	*hareket etmek*, to move
	yakıt (-tı), fuel
tip (-pi), type	*yüz*, face, surface
	kābiliyet (-ti), capability

4. Birleşik Amerika ordusunun sene sonuna kadar 1000 aded radarla idare edilen füzelere sahip olacağı açıklanmaktadır. (Nike) adı verilen bu füzeler seyir halinde iken hedefi kendiliğinden bulmakta ve tahribetmektedir. Yeni Meksiko'daki üsde* yapılan tecrübeler çok muvaffakiyetli olmuştur.

aded, (see § 91 (3))	*hedef*, target
idāre etmek, to direct	*tahribetmek*, to destroy
açıklamak, to reveal	*tecrübe*, experiment, test
seyir (-yri), motion, travel	*muvaffakiyet (-ti)*, success

5. Kuzey Atlantik Paktı teşkilâtı (NATO) Güney Avrupa Komutanlığı tarafından dün neşredilen tebliğde, beş millet deniz

* This is the locative of *üs*, ' base '. The *d*, in defiance of § 44, is to distinguish this word from *üste*, the dative of *üst*, ' top '.

ve hava birliklerinin Akdeniz'de, mayın salma, arama ve tarama
manevralarına başladıkları bildirilmektedir. Yunan birlikleri,
Yunanistan'ın NATO'ya girişindenberi, ilk defa olarak bu
manevralara katılmaktadır.

pakt (-*tı*), pact
teşkilât (-*tı*), organization
neşretmek, to publish
tebliğ, communiqué
Akdeniz, Mediterranean
salmak, to spread, lay

taramak, to comb
Yunan, Greek (qualifying noun:
   § 77)
Yunanistan, Greece
katmak, to add

KEY TO THE EXERCISES

Exercise 1

A. (1) From the bridge; of the houses; to the girl; from the money; on the steamer; to the buses. (2) We drank tea in the house. (3) I saw (some) girls; I saw the girls. (4) Ahmet went yesterday to Ankara. (5) I saw Ahmet yesterday on the bridge. (6) The steamer went from England to Turkey. (7) The bus went to Istanbul. (8) I took the coffee from the girl. (9) I saw a child on the steamer. (10) I gave the child an apple. (11) I gave the apple to a child. (12) The child went to the city.

B. (1) kahvede; vapurdan; İngilterede; köprüye; bir çocuktan. (2) Dün trende Ahmet'ten parayı aldım. (3) Kızlara çay verdim. (4) Çocuklara elmaları verdim. (5) Vapur, İstanbul'dan İngiltere'ye gitti. (6) Dün otobüste kızları gördüm. (7) Vapurda bir kahve içtik. (8) Çocuk, vapurdan trene gitti.

Exercise 2

A. (1) Has your father gone to the station? (2) Our friend's shop is in Galata, near to the police station (§ 65 (4)). (3) I saw him in the train, not in the bus. (4) I took a cigarette from my own box, not from yours. (5) I bought this book from your friend Ahmet. (6) This man's house is not far from the station, it is very near. (7) *He* went to the cinema yesterday evening; afterwards *we* drank coffee in our friends' house. (8) Is the new Director industrious?—No, he's not very industrious. (9) Their house is at Galata, isn't it?—Yes, near to the bridge. (10) I gave the box to this man, didn't I? (11) The child is in his room. He is in the child's room. (12) The neighbours' houses. The neighbours' house.

B. (1) Bu otomobil-i babanızdan aldım. Pek eski değil. (2) Eski müdür dün akşam Ankara'ya gitti, değil mi? (3) Kızım, arkadaşımızın dükkânına gitti. (4) Karakol, evimizden (bizim evden) uzak değildir. (5) Bu, sizin paranız değil. (6) Ben, bu akşam vapurda müdürün kız-ı-nı gördüm. (7) Kutunuz şimdi trende. (8) Onun işi pek mühim değil. (9) Arkadaşınız-ın babası pek çalışkan bir adamdır, değil mi? (10) Şimdi meşgul mü-sünüz?—Evet, pek meşgulüm.

Exercise 3

A. (1) We wanted to go to the Istanbul Exhibition, but we had no time. (2) The police officials didn't even look at my passport. (3) Your friends moved yesterday to another house, didn't they? (4) We waited-for you an hour this morning at the Islands quay; why didn't you come? (5) He wanted to buy cigarettes, but the shop was shut.—Wasn't there another shop? (6) There is an apple-tree in our garden, but this year it has given no fruit. (7) I saw your brother in the street, in an untidy get-up, coatless, hatless. (8) My bedroom is very damp. Is there an empty room in your hotel?—Unfortunately there isn't. (9) Is the tall child the Director's son?—No, he has a daughter, he has no son. (10) The Conqueror took Istanbul from the Byzantines in the year 1453. (11) The alcoholic drinks monopoly was one of the great works of the Republic (and) a principal source of profit of the State. (12) Haven't you read the book called *Our Village?*

B. (1) (Kız)kardeşiniz evli midir? (2) Başka bir otele gitmek istedi. (3) Bu sigara kutusu yeni mi?—Evet annem bana onu verdi. (4) Adresimizi belki telefon rehberinde buldu. (5) Elma ağaçlarımız bu yıl (sene) çok meyva verdi, değil mi? (6) Sarı-lı kız, Orhan'ın kardeş-i-dir. (7) Onu istasyonda bekledik fakat gelmedi. (8) Kızkardeşim evlerini (onların evini) almak istedi fakat ben beğenmedim, pek rutubetlidir. (9) Pasaportunuzu otelde mi bıraktınız? (10) Halk, memleketin gerçek (asıl) efendisidir.

Exercise 4

A. (1) Why aren't you going to the Islands to-day?—Because the weather isn't fine. (2) We were wanting to discuss this question with you. (3) My wife and I went round the Covered Market yesterday. (4) Did you come to Turkey by aeroplane or by steamer? (5) I've three tickets for this evening; you're coming with us, aren't you?—Unfortunately I've no time; I'm going to Ankara to-morrow morning (and) I want to go to bed early to-night. (6) On a rainy night, two horsemen were going along ('on') a lonely road. (7) I have not seen such a thing in my life. (8) There are 12 months in a year. There are 4 weeks in a month. There are 7 days in a week. The names of the days are these (following): Sunday, Monday, etc. Have you learned these (preceding)? (9) Is there a city in the world as beautiful as Istanbul? (10) It is necessary to send this letter by airmail.

B. (1) Karım, babasını görmek için Kıbrıs'a gitti. (2) Şu sarı saç-lı kız sizin kardeşiniz midir? (3) Babamla (babam ile) kardeşim yeni piyes-i beğenmedi(ler). (4) Kaç bilet almak isti-yorsunuz?—Beş tane. (5) Bir yılda (senede) üç yüz altmış beş gün vardır. (6) Yeni bakan bu sabah İstanbul'dan tayyare ile (uçakla) geliyor. (7) Bu su buz gibi-dir; bu su buz kadar soğuktur. (8) Niçin bu havada şapkasız paltosuz geziyorsunuz? (9) Maalesef kocam beni anlamıyor. (10) Şu adam-ı tanıyor musunuz? Niçin bize bakıyor?

Exercise 5

A. (1) You are going to strive, weary yourself and at last be successful. (2) Whose is the black car which-is-over-there?—I don't know; it's certainly not mine. (3) Where's your friend from?—He's like me, a Londoner. (4) Are you going to go to Turkey soon?—Not very soon; I shall go after the summer holiday. (5) Is your father going by to-day's train or is he staying over till ('remaining to') to-morrow? (6) Istanbul is both our biggest and our most beautiful city. (7) That picture is like the one in my room, isn't it?—Yes, but it's more beautiful than yours. (8) Why did you sit and not help me? (9) Of those two ladies, the one dressed in black is the Prime Minister's wife. (10) I wonder whether the Grand National Assembly will accept this motion?—It won't. (11) Weren't you going to speak of this problem? (12) This morning I got up before my brother.

B. (1) Yarınki toplantıdan dolayı tiyatroya gitmiyecektik. (2) Şu köşedeki adam ne yapıyor acaba?—Namaz kılıyor, değil mi? (3) Büyük Millet Meclisi (B.M.M.) Bakan-ın teklif-i-ni kabul etmedi mi? (4) Bizim iktisadi vaziyet (durum) şimdi bambaşkadır. (5) Tiyatrodan sonra İstasyon Lokantasına gittik. (6) Orhan, çocuklardan hem en büyüğü (§§ 43, 100 (1)) hem de en akıl-lı-sı-dır.—Kendi kızkardeş-i-nden daha akıllı mıdır acaba? (7) Bugünkü toplantıdan bahsediyor muydunuz? (8) Onun odası, benimki kadar temiz değil, benimki tertemizdir. (9) Çocuğu el-i-nden tuttum, Galata köprü-sü-nden beraber geçtik. (10) Sizin kardeş-iniz-in köpeğ-i-nin ism-i (ad-ı) nedir? —Onun köpeği yok, benimki-nin ismi Karabaş'tır. (11) Bence en güzel koku-lu çiçek güldür. (12) Nihayet geniş bahçeli bir ev bulduk.

Exercise 6

A. (1) Two teams of eleven people each. (2) You waited half an hour, we waited one and a half hours. (3) Who ate half of the bread? (4) I bought these oranges for four piastres each. The fruiterer wanted seven piastres each for some rather bigger ones ('for a-little more big-of-them'); I found (this) expensive and did not buy (them). (5) The banks give 2½% interest on ('to') small savings accounts. (6) The first snow of the year fell yesterday. (7) When did the last World War begin?—On 3rd September 1939. (8) I'll call again, perhaps to-morrow afternoon. (9) On 30th August 1922 the Turkish army won one of the world's greatest pitched battles. (10) Travelling in the sleeping-car is doubtless a very comfortable thing. (11) Whose are the papers on the third shelf? (12) I believe I trod on your foot. I beg your pardon, I didn't see.

B. (1) Lûtfen bana telefon rehberini getirir misiniz?—Hayhay!—Teşekkür ederim. (2) Yazı yazmak için kalem, kâğıt ve mürekkep lâzım. (3) Akşam-a kadar dolaştım, ayağıma göre bir ayakkabı bulmadım. (4) Hasta olmaktan korkmaz mısınız? (5) Biz tramvayı görür görmez, Orhan koşmağa başladı. (6) Saatiniz o dolabın ikinci rafında duruyor. (7) Ben bu sabah Taksim Meydanında tramvaya binerken, üç fotoğrafçı gördüm. (8) Bu apartıman tam size göre-dir. (9) Karı-m radyo-yu dinlerken dikiş diker. (10) İnsan tayyare ile (uçak ile, uçakla) kuş gibi havada uçar. (11) Her büyük şehir nesil-den nesl-e değişir. (12) O gitti, bilmem nereye?

Exercise 7

A. (1) The Bulgars are Turkish; it is the language which makes them Slav ('them Slav making is-language'). (2) Whom did you ask about this? (3) But this longing is not simply a feeling which belongs to time past. (4) Reach me that book. No, not that one, I want the (one) standing on that shelf. (5) Your friend is the how-manyeth of those standing in that file?—The sixth of them. (6) God protect the (one) remaining in the open in this season. (7) There are seven Mehmets in our Brigade; which-one-of-them are you enquiring about? (8) O Turkish youth, your first duty is to preserve and defend for ever Turkish independence and the Turkish Republic. (9) Wait-for me here; I'll come in five minutes. (10) Inside ten minutes we began to talk familiarly with him. (11) I want to wait-for my friends here; is it possible?—Of course it is, why shouldn't it be? ('why let it not be?'). (12) The view which meets ('strikes') your eye is the view of a natural fortification, with its pass between two flat hills.

B. (1) Köpek, ısıracak gibi dişlerini gösterdi. (2) O kadar hızlı yürümeyin. (3) Şu fotoğrafları al da benim masamın üzerine koy. (4) Şark için 'ölümün sırrına sahiptir' derler. (5) Kitabın yapraklarını parmakla değil, çakıyla açınız. (6) Hangi at birinci geldi? (7) Hamdolsun işimiz iyi gidiyor. (8) Geç kalmasın, erken gelsin. (9) Köyünden çıkmamış köylü bu meseleleri anlar mı?—Anlamaz. (10) Onlar bizden bir ev aşırı otururlar.

Exercise 8

A. (1) I have gone to Erzurum three times and by quite different routes each time ('at-the-three-of-them'). (2) Most of the girls who are entering now are very ugly. (3) This morning I bought two handkerchiefs. One of them is in my pocket, but what became of the other ('what it became') I don't know. (4) I saw no harm in-returning to ('on to') this topic. (5) The doctor went round the patients; he told off the nurse who forgot to give one patient's medicine at the proper time ('at its time'). (6) I am not accustomed to listening to gossip. (7) I am intending to go ('to-go I-am-in-the-intention-of-it') to Istanbul. Do you want to go too? (8) The moon becomes evident from its rising, the man from his walking. (9) Both the ministers of Vahdettin and Mustafa Kemal himself are seeking pretext(s) in order to cross over to Anatolia. (10) For this motherland what things have we not done! Some of us have died, some of us have made speeches.

B. (1) Saat sekize on var; saat sekize on kala; saat biri çeyrek geçiyor; saat biri çeyrek geçe; saat dokuz, dokuz buçuk sularında gelirler. (2) Bu eser, edebiyatımızda yer tutmıya lâyıktır. (3) Bugün Erzurum'a gitmekten vazgeçtim. (4) Beni dikkatle dinlemenizi rica ederim. (5) Bu yürüyüşle evlerine saat yediden evvel varmış olacağız. (6) Bu para bir altın saat almağa yetmez. (7) Bu iş beş dakka sürmez. (8) Bu, benim otomobilimi almanıza sebep teşkil eder mi? (9) Bu işi yapmanıza kim engel oldu? (10) İnsanlar yemek için yaşamazlar, yaşamak için yerler.

Exercise 9

A. (1) You will have read the article which came out in *Ulus* two days ago. You will have read it and been surprised. (2) Hush! Is that the way to talk in front of the child? ('Is that sort of talk spoken by the side of . . .?') (3) The newly built provincial government house will shortly be opened with a big ceremony. (4) A small piece of stick 10 centimetres long ('in the length of 10 centimetres') and 2 or 3 centimetres thick. (5) Two stones standing side by side with one metre interval. (6) Onto these stones a stick is placed, one and a half metres long, one or two centimetres in diameter. (7) They had received order(s) for the immediate arrest of the stranger ('about his being immediately arrested'). (8) You like the orange, but you've certainly never eaten one like this ('the-thus-of-it'). (9) General T.Y., who has (for) a long period served as commander of ('having done the commandership of') our Korea Combat Unit, is to be put on the retired list ('will-be-set-apart to-the-pensioned') next August. On the other hand ('from the other side, moreover'), Colonel C.D., who has served as Regimental Commander of our Korea Unit, will be promoted this year to the rank of Brigadier ('to-Brigadiership').

B. (1) Sinemayı tiyatroya daima tercih etmişimdir. (2) Bir günlük tren yolu uçakla bir buçuk saatte alınıyor. (3) Ben dün gece pencereden bakarken, kar yağdı. (4) Ben dün gece uyurken, kar yağmış. (5) Dün beni görmeğe gelmişsiniz; evde bulunmayışıma çok üzüldüm. (6) Dikensiz gül olmazmış. (7) Hayli yorulacaksınız. Çünkü bu, kolay başar-ıl-ır bir iş değildir. (8) Buradaki kum tepeleri bazı yerlerde altmış dokuz metreye kadar yükseliyordu. (9) Dört kere dokuz otuz altı eder. (10) Kendiniz-i üzmeyin.

Exercise 10

A. (1) The bad (part) of the business was this: this life had been lost, never more to return. (2) Are they not afraid of the coming of a day on which the account of these illegalities ('lawless-nesses') will be asked? (3) In the village, very few people know the official twelve months which are used in the city and which the villager calls 'the Government month'. (4) In London, the War Ministry spokesman said that this sort of news was no more than ('did not go forward from') a rumour. . . .

The American Ambassador said that he had no information ('his information not being') about this news-item. (5) The Beauty Queen of Turkey was chosen last night at the Atlas Cinema. The cinema auditorium had filled up early. A good many people too had lined up outside to see the beauties who were about to enter for the elections. (6) The villages which are our object of study (with the exception of one of them which is as much as fifty-five kilometres away) are within a 20–22-kilometre area round the city of Ankara. (7) One of the incongruities of our life is also that although we live and amuse ourselves in Beyoğlu, we don't like it, we find it ridiculous to mention it ('is our-not-liking . . . our-finding'). (8) A gang of people, with Turkish money in their hands, are currency-hunting ('are doing huntsmanship') and chasing tourists in the streets of Istanbul.

B. (1) Dün gece çok işim vardı, ancak saat birde yatabildim. (2) Uçun kuşlar doğduğum yere. (3) Umulmadık taş baş yarar. (4) Onlarda taklit edilemiyen şey giydikleri değil, giyinişleri idi. (5) Kendini göreceğim günü size de haber veririm. (6) Bugün gideceğim şüpheli-dir. (7) Bugünden yarını düşünmiyenler geleceğe emniyetle bakamazlar. (8) Bana yaptığınız bu iyiliği hiçbir zaman unutmıyacağım. (9) Sizin nasıl bir kumaş istediğinizi ben nerden bilirim? (10) Şehirden mandıralara giden yolun geçtiği tahta köprüde durdu . . . daldığı tatlı âlemden uyandı. Ne yaptığını, ne yapacağını bilmiyen bir adam gibiydi.

Exercise 11

A. (1) In the darkness of night we boarded the goods train, under the impression that it was the passenger train. (2) There must be a hole in the ball; it's always letting the air escape. (3) This jump caused him to lose his balance. (4) It means I've got to buy paper and pen and all the rest of it. (5) Those who were present looked-at-one another. (6) The persistence in these drinkers' wanting to make those-who-are beside-them drink too, is not comprehensible ('is not understood thing'). (7) Because he wrote a lot, they used to call Ahmet Mithat Efendi ' a machine of (§ 141) forty horse-power '. (8) In the last message received from the ship, it was reported ('in-the-act-of-being-made known ') that the ship had begun to be submerged in the waters. (9) Pasteur had discerned that, just as there was a virus producing ('giving birth to') every infectious disease ('ill-ness '), there would also be a virus of rabies. (10) The administration of the Sea Lines yesterday stopped the steamer ' Seyyar ' from (making its) voyage, by an order whose cause is not ('its cause-not-being') clear. The ' Seyyar ' will make its normal voyage on Saturday, the tickets sold for the steamer being valid. (11) They call the unit made up of 14 privates: ' section '. (12) You should walk on the right, not on the left.

B. (1) İş dün bitti; işi dün bitirdim. (2) Gazeteler-e bir ilân bas-tır-malı idik. (3) Raftan şu kitabı in-dir-ir misiniz?—Rafta kitap mitap yok. (4) Ne yapacağım diye düşünüyordum. (5) O, herkes-le pek resmî-dir. (6) Öteki oda bundan (daha) geniştir. (7) Denizaltı gemiyi bat-ır-dı. (8) Bana ihtiyac-ınız ol-up ol-ma-dığını öğrenmeğe geldim. (9) Yarın gelip beni görünüz. (10) Beni saat altı buçukta uyan-dır-ır mısınız?

Exercise 12

A. (1) England, which has the greater portion of her territories overseas, is in no position to neglect the sea ('is in the position pertaining-to-being-unable-to . . .'). (2) When a new bride is about to come to the house, if the rooms are not sufficient, a new room is added to the house. (3) If the weather doesn't clear by noon, we're not going out. (4) If he will take the trouble to open and read the last page, he will see this. (5) Even without the rest ('if the others were-not'), just this is sufficient. (6) If I had become accustomed to this pleasure, naturally it would come very hard now to give it up. (7) Whatever he says, nobody listens ('the listener does-not-occur'). (8) The works of this period, although they are not worthy of (a) great reliance, can be counted as *something*, in the midst of nothing ('existent in non-existence'). (9) If only he came and told me his trouble! I would find a remedy for it. (10) If this war would only stop and then . . .!—What will happen if it *does* stop? (11) If you look after it it will become an orchard, if you don't it will become a wilderness ('If you look, orchard comes into-being; if you do not look, mountain comes-into-being'). (12) Love him-who-loves thee, if-he-be level with the earth; don't-love him-who-does-not-love thee, if he be Sultan in Egypt.

B. (1) İyi-yle kötüyü ayır-acak yaştasınız. (2) Gitmem! . . . dediysem de, ısrar ettiler. (3) Bilmezse sorsun. (4) Kardeşim ise, oraya hiç gitmez. (5) Onun nasıl bir adam olduğunu bilseler. . . . (6) Saat bir-e kadar gelmezse siz beklemeyiniz.

(7) Sussanız a! Dinleseniz e! (8) Ne isterse yapar. (9) Hasan'ın bugün niçin okula gelmediğini bilse bilse Orhan bilir, git ondan sor. (10) Ne olursa olsun bu mektubu bitirmem lâzım.

Exercise 13

A. (1) For how much must one sell a cloth bought at 64 piastres a metre so that it may leave eight per cent profit on every metre? ('its-metre being-bought for 64 piastres a cloth for-how-much must-one-sell that in every metre-of-it in-the-hundred eight profit let-it-leave'). (2) This job will not end, unless you help too. (3) Since we've been married I've never heard him talking in his sleep. (4) Since the beginning of time ('since the world came into being'), the world has seen no catastrophe as great as the last war. (5) I hadn't intended to buy ('I had said let-me-not-buy') any more clothes, but now you see my friend's wedding has turned up ('come up'). (6) Pushing and shoving, we broke through the crowd and boarded the steamer. (7) I shall depart from this world and go, without learning what 'genius' means. (8) Naim Efendi shrugged his shoulders and bent his neck as if saying, 'What are we to do? Fate was thus.' (9) After his big sister returned from Europe, everything began to change. (10) Unless God grants ('God not-having-given'), what can the slave (i.e., mortal man) do? (11) Don't choose the radio which you are going to buy by the toss of a coin ('by-throwing heads-tails'). (12) I'll keep your place till you've smoked your cigarette.

B. (1) Güneş sönmedikçe hayat devam edecektir. (2) İstanbul gittikçe ağaçsız kalıyor. (3) Ben ancak elimdeki işi bit-ir-dik-ten sonra sizin yazı-nız-ı okuyabilirim. (4) Bir lokma ekmek (§ 140) yemeksizin yola çıkmıştık. (5) Yağmur yağdıkça hep o günü hatırla-r-ım. (6) Bir eve sahibinden izin almadan girilmez. (7) Camiin iki yüz metre kadar garbında (batısında) yeni yapılan bir çeşme bulunmaktadır. (8) İtiraz etmeksizin (etmeden) dediğimi kabul etti. (9) Saat yedi buçuğu geçmiş; çabuk olalım, geç kalacağız. (10) Ben size hangi gün geleyim?

Exercise 14

(1) Let-us-not-talk as-if-quarrelling. (2) It turns out that we have been nurturing snakes in our bosom! (3) I am grieved while departing from A., just as my departure from I. made me sad ('had given me sadness'). (4) (I gather that) you were expect-

ing me for dinner, whereas I had no news of this invitation. (5) And what about your big sister? Won't she be coming? (6) It's too bad of you, (my) Teacher; I should never have expected this of you!—Nothing wrong I hope, my son? What has happened? (7) You at least should not have spoken thus. (8) So he's pushed his nose too into this business, has he? (9) Mind you don't forget what I say. (10) If once he sees, we've had it. (11) He was pretty well thrown out; we were saying, ' He won't come any more after this '; and now you see he's come again. (12) Everyone has gone, only he has remained. (13) May his eye come out! (14) This is an unnecessary question, isn't it? (i.e., Need you ask?) (15) The children's clothes must be cut rather full. (16) There was a certain acidity (' a sour-ish-ness ') in their manner which showed that they were not pleased at (' from ') my coming. (17) A thing's being cheap or dear does not always depend on the price it costs. (18) The official whose turn came (' his-turn coming the-official ') used to be promoted automatically. According to what we learn, under (' in ') the new Bill, officials will be promoted according to merit, not according to time; if need arises they will even be able to be promoted three times in one year.

Exercise 15

(1) With whatever weapons he arms himself let him arm himself, he will not be able to escape from death (i.e., let him arm himself as he pleases). (2) Oh dear! Things have got complicated! (3) We went round from door to door (' door door ') and sought him. (4) Last night one of my grandfather's sheep lambed. (5) He folded the letter into (' to ') two in order to put it into the envelope. (6) The weather's getting cloudy. I expect it's going to rain. (7) One person was missing; now we're up to strength (' we-have-completed-ourselves '). (8) I want to wire there for them to send (' for their-sending ') my things. (9) They call people who have no employment (' his-work his-toil not-being ') and roam here and there, ' Pavement Engineer ' (i.e., tramp, cf. our ' milestone inspector '). (10) The unbound parts of this book are sold for 50 k. less (' for the deficiency of 50 k. ') than the bound version (' than-the bound-of-it '). (11) Manuscript and print, all kinds of old books are bought. Books in large quantity are bought on the spot (' in-its-place '), a man being sent. Application to our office (' administration-house ') in person or by

letter. (12) The games and library rooms of the building are to be kept open as formerly for the benefit of the young ('youth'). (13) My grandfather fell-asleep-suddenly while reading his newspaper. (14) You are comparing these two things but this comparison which you are making is not appropriate. For the things which you are comparing ('pertaining-to-your-making their-comparison') are not of the same species. (15) Those who have finished the age of six by the end of September every year are obliged to continue at elementary ('first') school until the end of the school year in which they complete ('pertaining-to their completing') the age of fourteen. (16) Rather than to run after an impossible thing ('a work which will-not-be'), it is doubtless more reasonable at once to-taste-quickly the pleasure of life wherever one finds it ('in-the-place pertaining-to-its-passing to-the hand'). (17) According to what has been made known from reliable sources, the Varna Consulate having been transferred to the Sofia Consulate, the two Consulates have been amalgamated ('made-to-become-one'). (18) She used often to be taken ill and as soon as the fever began she would rave-about the waters of Istanbul.

Military Extracts

1. Under cover of a heavy artillery barrage, the Reds had attacked a 4-kilometre front which the Turkish Brigade and the 35th American Regiment were holding. Allied artillery and mortars, with the barrage fire which they opened, stopped the Communists some 80 metres away from the United Nations lines. After a violent engagement which lasted two hours, the Reds withdrew.

2. It has been confirmed that ('according to what is confirmed') the Regimental Commander Colonel Nuri Pamir, who was inspecting the front-line fortifications of the Turkish Brigade which is fighting in Korea for the sake of the ideal of United Nations, was killed ('became martyr') on Thursday 5th June as the result of a piece of shrapnel's hitting his skull, as the result of the enemy artillery fire which was opened.

3. Up to last year, it was suggested that atom bombs could be used ('their-future-being-able-to-be-used was suggested') only in the strategic sphere (and) that their use ('their-being-used') in the tactical sphere would be dangerous not only for the enemy but also for (one's) own units. Now, however ('as for now'), it is

revealed that a good many types of atomic weapons and bombs have (been) begun to be made, including ('as far as') tactical atomic weapons which infantry, too, will be able to use. . . . Next, it is revealed that the manufacture has begun of aircraft carriers driven by ('moving by') atomic energy, submarines driven by atomic energy (and) war-planes driven by atomic energy, and that these aircraft carriers will be capable of going round the world ('will be in-the-capability pertaining to future-being-able-to-go . . .') without-taking fuel from anywhere, and these submarines (ditto) without coming up at all to the sea surface.

4. It is revealed that by the year-end the U.S. Army ('the army of United America') will possess 1000 radar-directed rockets. These rockets, which have been named 'Nike' ('the name of N. being-given these rockets'), find the target of their own accord while in flight ('while in the state of motion') and destroy it. Tests carried out at the base in New Mexico have been highly successful.

5. In the communiqué published yesterday by the Southern Europe Command of the North Atlantic Pact organization (NATO), it is announced that sea and air units of five nations have begun mine-laying and -sweeping manœuvres in the Mediterranean. For the first time since Greece's entry into NATO, Greek forces are joining ('are being added to') these manœuvres.

INDEX OF SUFFIXES

Of suffixes liable to the fourfold vowel-harmony, only the forms in *i* are shown; of those liable to the twofold harmony, only the forms in *e*. If you find an unaccountable *i*, *ı*, *ü* or *u* before *y*, remember that it may be for an original *e* or *a* (§ 88, *Note*). The buffer-letter *y* is not shown. Suffixes which may begin with *c* or *ç*, *d* or *t*, will be found under *c* and *d*. Thus, if you are looking up the suffixes of *bakamıyarak*, you will have to seek the *-yarak* under *-erek*, the *-amı-* under *-eme*. For the *-tur* of *bozuktur*, see *-dir*; for the *-yı* of *Ankara'yı*, see *-i*; for the *-sün* of *görsün*, see *-sin*; for the *-ça* of *hoşça*, see *-ce*. The numbers refer to paragraphs. See also §§ 174, 175.

ADVERTISING & PUBLICITY   ALGEBRA   AMATEUR ACTING   ANAT
BOOK-KEEPING   BRICKWORK   BRINGING UP CHILDREN   BUSINES
CHESS   CHINESE   COMMERCIAL ARITHMETIC   COMMERCIAL ART
COMPOSE MUSIC   CONSTRUCTIONAL DETAILS   CONTRACT BRIDGE
SPEEDWORDS   ECONOMIC GEOGRAPHY   ECONOMICS   ELECTR
ENGLISH GRAMMAR   LITERARY APPRECIATION   ENGLISH RENASCE
REVIVAL   VICTORIAN AGE   CONTEMPORARY LITERATURE   ETCHIN
FREELANCE WRITING   FRENCH   FRENCH DICTIONARY   FRENCH
LIVING THINGS   GEOLOGY   GEOMETRY   GERMAN   GERMAN
GOOD CONTROL OF INSECT PESTS   GOOD CONTROL OF PLANT DISEA
GOOD FARMING BY MACHINE   GOOD FARM WORKMANSHIP   GOO
GOOD MARKET GARDENING   GOOD MILK FARMING   GOOD PIG KE
GOOD ENGLISH   GREEK   GREGG SHORTHAND   GUIDEBOOK TO T
GREAT   BOLIVAR   BOTHA   CATHERINE THE GREAT   CHATHAM   CLEM
LIBERALISM   HENRY V   JOAN OF ARC   JOHN WYCLIFFE   LENIN   LOUIS
ROBES   HASTINGS
HOUS   REPAIRS
WRITE   ND TOO
MECH   **GIVE INSTRUCTION**   LCRAFT
MOTO   FICIENC
PHYSI   **TO A WISE MAN...**   DESIGN
ADMI   NG   R
PHR   OOK   SAILING   SALESMANSHIP   SECRET   ACTICE
DEBAT   SPELLING   STAMP COLLECTING   STUDE   DE   S
TYPEWRITING   USE OF GEOGRAPHY   WAY TO POETR   WR
COOKERY FOR GIRLS   DOGS AS PETS FOR BOYS AND GIRLS   KNI
PHOTOGRAPHY FOR BOYS AND GIRLS   RADIO FOR BOYS   RIDING
SOCCER FOR BOYS   STAMP COLLECTING FOR BOYS AND GIRLS   WO
ACTING   ANATOMY   ARABIC   ASTRONOMY   BANKING   BE
CHILDREN   BUSINESS ORGANISATION   CALCULUS   CANASTA
COMMERCIAL ART   COMMERCIAL CORRESPONDENCE   COMMER
CONTRACT BRIDGE   COOKING   CRICKET   DRAWING   DRES
ECONOMICS   ELECTRICITY   ELECTRICITY IN THE HOUSE   ELOCU
ENGLISH RENASCENCE   ENGLISH RENASCENCE TO THE ROMANTI
LITERATURE   ETCHING   EVERYDAY FRENCH   TO EXPRESS YOUR
DICTIONARY   FRENCH PHRASE BOOK   GARDENING   GAS IN
GERMAN   GERMAN DICTIONARY   GERMAN GRAMMAR   GERMA
CONTROL OF PLANT DISEASES   GOOD FARM ACCOUNTING   G
GOOD FARM WORKMANSHIP   GOOD FRUIT FARMING   GOOD GR
GOOD MILK FARMING   GOOD PIG KEEPING   GOOD POULTRY KE
GREGG SHORTHAND   GUIDEBOOK TO THE BIBLE   HINDUSTANI
CATHERINE THE GREAT   CHATHAM   CLEMENCEAU   CONSTANTINE C
ARC   JOHN WYCLIFFE   LENIN   LOUIS XIV   MILTON   PERICLES   PETER
USE OF HISTORY   WARREN HASTINGS   WOODROW WILSON   HOC
HOUSEHOLD ELECTRICITY   HOUSE REPAIRS   ITALIAN   JOINER
MANAGEMENT   MATHEMATICS   HAND TOOLS   ENGINEERIN
DRAUGHTSMANSHIP   METEOROLOGY   MODELCRAFT   MODERN DA
MUSIC   NORWEGIAN   PERSONAL EFFICIENCY   PHILOSOPHY   PH
SHORTHAND   PLANNING AND DESIGN   PLUMBING   POLISH   P